WHEN GOD SHOWS UP

STAYING READY FOR THE UNEXPECTED

R. T. KENDALL

Renew

A Division of Gospel Light
Ventura, California, U.S.A.

Published by Renew Books
A Division of Gospel Light
Ventura, California, U.S.A.
Printed in U.S.A.

Renew Books is a ministry of Gospel Light, an evangelical Christian publisher dedicated to serving the local church. We believe God's vision for Gospel Light is to provide church leaders with biblical, user-friendly materials that will help them evangelize, disciple and minister to children, youth and families.

It is our prayer that this Renew book will help you discover biblical truth for your own life and help you meet the needs of others. May God richly bless you.

For a free catalog of resources from Renew Books and Gospel Light. Please call your Christian supplier, or contact us at 1-800-4-GOSPEL *or at* www.gospellight.com.

This book was first published as *Ready for God?* in 1995 by Scripture Union in London, England.

Cover Design by Kevin Keller
Interior Design by Mario Ricketts
Edited by Virginia Woodard

Library of Congress Cataloging-in-Publication Data

Kendall, R. T.
[Ready for God]
When God shows up : staying ready for the unexpected / R. T. Kendall.
     p.   cm.
Originally published: Ready for God. London : Scripture union. 1995.
ISBN 0-8307-2340-4 (pbk.)
1. Spiritual life—Christianity.   I. Title.
   BV4501.2.K4289 1998

                                 248.4—dc2198-38665

                                       CIP

1 2 3 4 5 6 7 8 9 10 11 12 13 14 15 16 17 18 19 20 / 04 03 02 01 00 99 98
Rights for publishing this book in other languages are contracted by Gospel Literature International (GLINT). GLINT also provides technical help for the adaptation, translation and publishing of Bible study resources and books in scores of languages worldwide. For further information, write to GLINT at P.O. Box 4060, Ontario, CA 91761-1003, U.S.A. You may also send e-mail to Glintint@aol.com, or visit their web site at www.glint.org.

TO
HARRY AND KIMBERLEY
AND
JOHN AND MICHELLE

CONTENTS

FOREWORD

You are about to experience a beautiful collision between the classic and the contemporary! In fact, in a very real sense, that's not only what may be *said* about this book, but it *is* also what this book *says*.

For example, nothing is more "classic" than our Creator's unlimited creative potential, nor anything more "contemporary" than humankind's obvious human limitations. Before you have read very far, you are going to be encouraged to let those two collide—to welcome the wonder-working wisdom of our Creator into whatever need characterizes your own present moment.

God *is* "showing up" today! He's revealing Himself and manifesting His power in remarkable and amazing ways—and hungry souls are the primary candidates for experiencing His arrival after that fashion. R. T. Kendall is someone who is beautifully qualified to point the path for any of us with that "hunger and thirst for righteousness" because he has led his congregation in that way—and not without a price.

Any spiritual leader who pursues the Spirit's present workings with passion, while still staying true to tradition's proven values with fidelity, will experience a collision. He pays the price of being stuck between the fanatic and the formalist. He never seems to completely please the radical revivalist or the trustworthy traditionalist. But if you can find a leader who presses for the best of today's *newness* while still holding to the best of yesterday's *solidity*, you'll make a discovery. You'll find refreshing and renewal that not only *stirs* your soul with heavenly excitement, but will also *stabilize* your path forward toward longer-term growth and blessing.

In regard to refreshing us with revival hope, this book is alive and intensely practical. But I have enjoyed this book for another reason. It has to do with a less observable "collision" than mentioned earlier, but that contributes to making these pages a source of lasting value to the reader. It relates to something that, I suppose, only a pastor might notice.

You, dear reader, are about to enter the collision zone where two *preaching* values encounter one another. You will unquestionably notice—immediately—the way these pages speak to *you*. The insights reaching into your heart are not only practical, but also intensely personal. Dr. Kendall's stories, illustrating the texts he unfolds, are in the best tradition of today's contemporary Christian writer. However, there is an almost silent "crash" as this fact is impacted by another.

For earnest Bible teachers, the "handling" of a text is as important as the "proclaiming" of its truth. This is a classic value that is too often neglected by (sometimes even unknown to) some current messengers of God's Word. It doesn't mean that these are teaching errors, but that their *exposition*—the actual unlocking of the *inside* of the Bible text—is sometimes incomplete. In contrast to this too-common "contemporary" failing, Pastor Kendall brings that classic expositional approach that is so historic in British tradition.

The first decade of my pastoral life, I was greatly influenced by the writings of some of the great expositors of the English pulpit. Among these were G. Campbell Morgan, Reginald E. O. White and Guy H. King, three preachers of the twentieth century, but who evidenced the qualities born of earlier insightful teaching resulting from thorough scholarship. That classic quality needs to impact even more contemporary Christian resources, for—as you're about to see—there is a richness and depth that such solid study gives to us all.

This enriching quality is actually unsurprising in one sense. Dr. Kendall is pastor of Westminster Chapel, where he opens the

Word at a pulpit with a long history of faithful, gifted preachers—a role he serves worthily. But even more important than his
preaching, I am impressed with his passion.

This is a book filled with the Holy Spirit of revival! Though
this book is the fruit of careful study, it is light-years removed
from being stuffy. It is center in the current of the Spirit's flow-
ing renewed life and blessing into the Church today. All in all, it's
"the right stuff"—the kind of food for the soul that both *builds*
and *blesses*. Like the United States astronaut training program
that gave rise to "the right stuff" term, I think you're on the
brink of "liftoff"—ready to gain a new outlook from a new level
of perspective.

But the difference is, there is nothing "spacey" about this
"stuff." You'll be lifted to the heavens, but you're going to find
yourself experiencing the kind of thing that keeps your feet on
the ground—and makes true revival something that is down-to-
earth and abidingly real.

Jack W. Hayford, D.Litt.
Senior Pastor
The Church On The Way
Van Nuys, California

PREFACE

My hobby is bonefishing, a sport that is well known in the Florida Keys. Before coming to England, I managed to go bonefishing once of twice a week—but this is now limited to our vacation time in August. Through the Island Community Church in Islamorada, Florida, we met some of the loveliest people on the face of the earth. Among them are Harry Spear and John Sutter, who are bonefish guides—the best. They realize I cannot afford their fees, but they take me out from time to time in exchange for my answering their theological questions (for which they have a deep hunger and thirst).

I take great pleasure in dedicating this book to Harry and John and their wives. It happens that one of their heroes is Jack Hayford. They will be thrilled that their names and his appear on the same page, and I am honored that Jack has kindly written a foreword. I am better known in our mother country than in my own, and I hope that this highly esteemed man of God will open doors for a wider readership.

The people of Regal have been very kind to me. I am happy to be associated with them. My deep thanks also go to my secretary Sheila Penton who typed the manuscript. I will never forget the particularly helpful criticisms and suggestions made by Allison Barr.

My deepest gratitude, as always, is to my wife, Louise. May God bless all who read this little book.

R. T. Kendall
Westminster Chapel
Buckingham Gate
London SW1
June 1998

INTRODUCTION

My family and I came to England from the United States on September 1, 1973. I came to do theological research at Regent's Park College, Oxford, and finished approximately three years later. Except for taking my oral exam, we were completely prepared to return to the United States. We had shipped our books, clothes, souvenirs and my son's new bicycle to our home in Florida. While waiting for my oral exam, I accepted an invitation to preach at Westminster Chapel. They asked me to stay. We eventually agreed. My ministry in London began February 1, 1977.

It has not been easy. But without any doubt, the best thing that has happened to me is that I have been forced to know God in a way that, if I am totally honest, probably would have eluded me had we returned to the United States. Forced? I fear so. Had we returned to the United States, I suspect that an easier way of life would have permitted me to maintain a status quo relationship with God. Not that my relationship with God was totally unsatisfactory; it is simply that I doubt I would have been constrained to seek God's face as I have had to do here in England.

God knows what it takes to get our attention. You could not have told me God didn't have my full attention in 1973—or in 1977. But the past twenty-five years have been met with my worst suffering, greatest frustrations and bitterest disappointments. The result for me has been a willingness not only to seek God's face with all my heart, but also to become open to Him as I had never been. Neither could you have told me I wasn't open to Him. Indeed, I was—as far as I knew. But God has a way of showing us depths of His ways that—at least in my case—we would not have encountered apart from fairly severe suffering and disciplining.

The insights of this book represent some of the fringe benefits of being forced to listen to God in a way I had not previously envisaged. The big surprise for me was to discover the unexpected ways by which God not only gets our attention, but also manifests Himself. If God doesn't have our attention, we could completely miss seeing His glory—right before our eyes—and we would not even know He had shown up!

You could never have convinced the chief priests of Israel two thousand years ago that Messiah could appear before their eyes and they would not recognize Him, but they missed Him. You could never have told the Pharisees they would miss God's Messiah, but they did. I fear many sincere Christians are in the same boat. We all have our fears and prejudices, and if what God is up to doesn't cohere with our comfort zone, we usually miss Him entirely and feel no pain.

In May 1994, I felt led to introduce a Prayer Covenant to the members of Westminster Chapel. This wasn't the first of such; several years before, a Prayer Covenant in a time of crisis carried us to the sweetest unity of any church I have known. But in 1994, we were keen to see God work—so much so that one of the petitions was this:

We pray for the manifestation of the glory of God in our midst, along with an ever-increasing openness in us to the manner in which He chooses to turn up.

The rationale for this petition was this: I know enough about church history to realize that God not only manifests Himself in a variety of ways, but He also has a strange habit of doing what He has never done before. Not only that, He loves to show up in a way that offends the sophisticated! I was so desirous for God to work in Westminster Chapel that I felt I must prepare the people for the unusual—should God want to show up in a strange sort of way.

On May 26, 1994, I finalized the five petitions in the new

Prayer Covenant and ordered that they be printed and ready for distribution on Sunday, June 5. On May 31, my close friend Lyndon Bowring, Charlie Colchester and I went to see the film *Schindler's List* in Leicester Square, London. Just before the film, we enjoyed a Chinese dinner on Gerrard Street in Soho.

While we were being served, Charlie spoke up: "Have you heard about the blessing of the Holy Spirit in Toronto?" We hadn't. "Well, I hardly know where to begin. The strangest things happened at our church [St. Paul's, Onslow Square, where Charlie is church warden] last Sunday. When people were prayed for, they fell to the floor, laughing. We left the church at 11 o'clock at night with at least fifty bodies lying there." He then told us more about this phenomenon, which had also recently appeared in Holy Trinity, Brompton, a lively Anglican (Episcopalian) church in Knightsbridge. He felt fairly certain it was of the Holy Spirit, although he was aware of how strange it all seemed.

Lyndon and I had our questions. I felt in my heart that this thing wasn't of God, but I recall in that moment a sense of sobriety that was more intense than anything I experienced during the movie we later went to see.

The following Sunday, June 5, I introduced "Prayer Covenant 1994," making the five petitions the points of my morning sermon. When I came to the third petition, previously quoted, I mentioned what is now called the "Toronto Blessing." It was the first time that most of those present had ever heard about it. I said, "If you put me under a lie detector and asked me if I believe that this is of God, I would have to say no." However, I used the Toronto Blessing as an illustration of what I meant by being open to the manner in which God *chooses* to show up. "After all," I said, "what if it *is* of God? Are we prepared for God to turn up *like that?*"

To me, it served only as a timely illustration of what I meant by openness, nothing more. I didn't think it was of God, partly, I fear, because I didn't *want* it to be of God. For one thing, I dreaded God being involved in anything weird. For another—and this gets closer to the bone—I dreaded God doing anything like this unless He did it in our church first!

A few days later, a close friend, a reformed Baptist minister, came to see me in my study for coffee. When he arrived, I told him I had also invited the Reverend Bob Cheesman to come in and pray for me. Bob had recently returned from Toronto and was full of excitement about the blessing he himself had received. My friend hadn't heard of the Toronto Blessing until that moment. I said to him, "You can watch while Bob prays for me." I had claimed to be open minded about it, and I now wanted to prove I was by opening my heart to be prayed for by someone who had been to Toronto. My friend replied, skeptical and not very enthusiastic, "Oh well, he can pray for me too, if he wants."

Bob knocked on the door seconds later, and was followed in by another friend of mine whose name is Gerald Coates. Gerald didn't know Bob had come to pray for me. But the four of us stood and prayed. In less than thirty seconds, my friend fell forward to the floor and lay motionless for at least ten minutes. I was impressed. The "blessing" had bypassed me and gone to him! He told me the following week that he had felt an unusual sense of God, which lasted for several days, unlike he had ever known.

The next day I had lunch with Ken Costa, a leading layman from Holy Trinity, Brompton. Given what had spontaneously happened the day before in my study, and after hearing the things Ken related, I knew I would have to climb down from my view that the Toronto phenomenon was not of God. I feared the worst—that it just might be of God. "God's feather," Ken said to me, "it is only a touch, and only the beginning."

This book is not about the Toronto Blessing, which, nonetheless, serves as an illustration of what I mean by being ready for the way God can show up. I now believe that the blessing *is* of God. I believe that God can show up in many different ways and at unexpected times. That is what the following chapters attempt to show.

ANSWERED PRAYER

Then an angel of the Lord appeared to him, standing at the right side of the altar of incense. When Zechariah saw him, he was startled and was gripped with fear. But the angel said to him: "Do not be afraid, Zechariah; your prayer has been heard. Your wife Elizabeth will bear you a son, and you are to give him the name John. He will be a joy and delight to you, and many will rejoice because of his birth, for he will be great in the sight of the Lord. He is never to take wine or other fermented drink, and he will be filled with the Holy Spirit even from birth. Many of the people of Israel will he bring back to the Lord their God. And he will go on before the Lord, in the spirit and power of Elijah, to turn the hearts of the fathers to their children and the disobedient to the wisdom of the righteous—to make ready a people prepared for the Lord."

Zechariah asked the angel, "How can I be sure of this?
I am an old man and my wife is well along in years."

The angel answered, "I am Gabriel. I stand in the presence of God, and I have been sent to speak to you and to
tell you this good news. And now you will be silent and
not able to speak until the day this happens, because you
did not believe my words, which will come true at their
proper time" (Luke 1:11-20).

May I begin by asking a question: Are you ready for answered
prayer?

Many years before these events described in Luke, a young
couple—Zechariah and Elizabeth—had prayed for a son.
Unexpectedly, one day, as Zechariah is ministering as a priest in
the Temple, the angel Gabriel appears, and says, "Do not be
afraid, Zechariah; your prayer has been heard." Zechariah is
nearly scared to death.

What would our reaction be? If the Lord sent an angel to say
to you, "I've got instructions to tell you your prayer has been
heard," would you say, "Prayer? What prayer?" Or would you say,
"Well, I know what that is!"?

The background is this. Perhaps twenty or thirty years earlier,
shortly after Zechariah and Elizabeth were married, they wondered why God had given them no children. It turned out that
Elizabeth was barren. Sometimes God strategically closes the
womb of a woman in order to drive a couple to prayer. In the
same way, God can strategically "close the womb" of a church to
drive that church to prayer. We know that in this case Zechariah
and Elizabeth had no choice but to go to God. Abraham had done
this when Sarah and he were childless, as had Isaac and Rebekah,
and so had Hannah. Now Zechariah and Elizabeth pray for a son,
but the years go by, and there's no sign at all that God is going to
answer their prayer. So they let that prayer request fade away—
they just know it's one God isn't going to answer.

In the meantime, Zechariah has the privilege of being a priest in Israel. We don't know how many priests there were at the time; we are told ten thousand at least. Because there were so many, the only way to have the honor of burning incense in the Temple was to be chosen by lot. And that's what happens. Zechariah is chosen by lot to burn incense in the Temple—a very high honor. We can be sure it is a day he has looked forward to, and it's obvious from the context that he has all his friends there. They are holding him up in prayer and waiting to find out the results. This is the moment God chooses! Zechariah isn't anticipating anything supernatural taking place. The burning of incense in the Temple is just a ritual. But suddenly God appears.

It's interesting. Sometimes in God's strategy He will work coincidentally, and sometimes He works according to what we today would call the "church calendar." For example, the Day of Pentecost—when so many Jews from throughout the Mediterranean were in Jerusalem to celebrate that important feast—was a strategic opportunity for Him (see Acts 2:1-5). It's as if God said, "What a good day to pour out My Spirit"—and Christianity began to spread like wildfire. Never be surprised if on a special day God does something unusual.

It was a special day for Zechariah in the Temple, but he wasn't prepared. He didn't know he was a "sovereign vessel," that is, one chosen to do an unusual work for God. God uses sovereign vessels today. You may think, *Well, He wouldn't use me like that! I'm a nobody.* But you see, God has a sense of humor! The kind of person who feels he or she couldn't possibly be chosen is just the kind of person God loves to choose.

So Zechariah is to be a sovereign vessel, the father of one who "in the spirit and power of Elijah" would "turn the hearts of the fathers to their children," and the disobedient to the wisdom of the righteous (Malachi 4:6).

The angel, Gabriel, says, "Your prayer has been heard."

Zechariah says, "Prayer? What prayer?"

CHAPTER ONE

"Oh," says the angel, "you and Elizabeth prayed for a son."

"Oh, *that* prayer! Well," says Zechariah, "that was twenty-five, thirty years ago."

"Well, your prayer has been heard. Your wife Elizabeth will conceive."

"It's not possible," says Zechariah. "Have you had a look at my wife lately? She's past the age of bearing a child."

ARE YOU READY FOR GOD?

Zechariah wasn't ready. Are *you* ready for God? Are you waiting for God to answer prayer? Are there prayers that you have long since taken off your prayer-request list because you were sure God wasn't going to answer them? There are two important principles here.

Any Prayer Prayed in the Will of God Will Be Answered

How do we know this? Because the Bible says so: "This is the confidence we have in approaching God: that if we ask anything according to his will, he hears us" (1 John 5:14).

When the Bible says God "hears us," it reflects a Hebraic way of thinking. In the Hebrew language the word *shema* means "to hear"; it also means "to obey." Every Jewish person knows the Shema: "Hear, O Israel: the Lord our God is one Lord." Sometimes a mother will say to her child, "Did you hear me?" implying, "You obviously didn't because you're not obeying." However, when the word *shema* is used, hearing is the same thing as obeying—if you hear, you obey. So when it says, "If we ask anything according to [God's] will, he hears us," it means He will obey our request, if that request is in His will. You can never *make* God do anything that isn't in His will; but if you ask according to His will, He hears.

Of course, there's a problem. We don't always know that we *are* praying in God's will. If only we did! As soon as we had asked for something we could say, "Ah, I prayed in the will of God!" John says, "This is the confidence we have in approaching God: that if we ask anything according to his will, he hears us. And if we know that he hears us—whatever we ask—we know that we have what we asked of him" (1 John 5:14,15). You see, it's a big "if" when He says, "*if* we know that he hears us": it implies that we don't always know.

Now there are times when I make a request to God and I know I'm heard. I *know* it. I'm sorry to say it doesn't happen often, and you may think, *Well, if you were more spiritual it would happen to you all the time!* But let's think a moment. Is there any question about the apostle Paul's spirituality? Listen to what he says in Romans 8:26: "The Spirit helps us in our weakness. We do not know what we ought to pray for, but the Spirit himself intercedes for us with groans that words cannot express." The point is that the Holy Spirit intercedes for us, but He doesn't tell us what He is saying to God.

If you have ever lived in a rural area, you may have picked up the telephone, heard someone talking, and had to put down the phone and wait your turn because it was a party line. My wife, Louise, my son, T. R., my daughter, Melissa, and I used to live in Salem, Indiana, out in the country in the middle of nowhere. We had eleven people on our party line! It was a miracle if you could get a dial tone because you just expected to hear somebody talking. Once I lifted up the phone and heard someone talking about *me*. It was kind of embarrassing: I didn't like what I was hearing and I gently put down the receiver.

What if we could pick up a divine telephone and hear the Holy Spirit talking about us? We could hear exactly what the

Holy Spirit was saying to the Father as He interceded for us? The trouble is, we can't: "The Spirit himself intercedes for us with groans that words cannot express" (Romans 8:26). That means we wouldn't understand what the Holy Spirit was actually saying. But it would be wonderful if we could tune in. Then, if we *knew* what He was saying, we could say, "Fine, I'll accept that. That's what I want."

The trouble is that big "if"—*if* we know His will. You can pray in the will of God and not know it. Zechariah and Elizabeth prayed in the will of God. They didn't know it. Because God didn't jump to answer their prayer the first time, they just assumed it wasn't God's will. Let's think back on our own prayer requests, maybe for last year, maybe going back before then. Think of one prayer that hasn't been heard, as far as you know, that you have long since given up praying. What's the principle to apply? That any prayer prayed in the will of God will be answered. So what's the problem?

**The Shape Answered Prayer Takes Is
Determined by Our Readiness at the Time**
It turns out—how sad it is—that Zechariah wasn't ready. He wanted to argue with the angel. Do you know why he wanted to argue? Because *he* wasn't right spiritually. Which shows that a person can be involved in the work of ministry even if his heart isn't right. When our hearts aren't right, we want to argue with God. Zechariah's day had come, and the Lord appeared. The angel delivered His good news, but because Zechariah didn't believe it, He had to go on, "And now you will be silent and not able to speak until the day this happens, because you did not believe my words."

Listen! *Any prayer prayed in the will of God will be answered, but the shape answered prayer takes is determined by our readiness at the time*—and Zechariah wasn't ready. All those friends who had come to pray for him while he was inside the

Temple are excited to know what has happened. He comes out—and he can't speak! It's embarrassing. On top of that, in a few months his wife *is* pregnant. His friends think it's wonderful! They come to see Zechariah and Elizabeth and say, "Zechariah, we're so happy for you. We're so proud of you! Your wife's going to have a baby! We know this is what you've always wanted."

Zechariah replies, "Mmm mmmm." He's humiliated.

I can remember many years ago, back in Ashland, Kentucky, when a couple felt led to start a new church in the south part of Ashland. Many people opposed the idea, and there were some who laughed at them. The couple rented a garage in which to hold services, and eventually there were as many as eleven attending, but people still laughed and scoffed. However, that little group prayed hard for numbers and a new building. They prayed that God would give them their own church.

Do you know, that prayer was answered! Some years later, one of the most beautiful buildings in that part of Ashland was erected. The day came for the dedication, and they brought in the general superintendent of their denomination especially for it. The new building was packed with more than three hundred people.

That's not the end of the story, however. The very man whose vision it was to start that church had, in the meantime, fallen into sin and bitterness. Things were so bad that he wasn't even welcome at the dedication service. The nearest he could get was to drive past the church that day and take a glance. His prayer was answered, but he himself wasn't ready.

Are we ready for answered prayer? Zechariah's story should give us encouragement to go back and start praying again. It's a wonderful, wonderful thing to be ready when God appears. When we're not ready, what should have been our finest hour will, instead, be under a cloud.

WHEN
GOD SHOWS UP

When he came near the place where the road goes down the Mount of Olives, the whole crowd of disciples began joyfully to praise God in loud voices for all the miracles they had seen:

"Blessed is the king who comes in the name of the Lord!"

"Peace in heaven, and glory in the highest!"

Some of the Pharisees in the crowd said to Jesus, "Teacher, rebuke your disciples!"

"I tell you," he replied, "if they keep quiet, the stones will cry out."

As he approached Jerusalem and saw the city, he wept over it and said, "If you, even you, had only known on this day what would bring you peace—but now it is hidden from your eyes. The days will come upon you when your enemies will build an embankment against you and encircle you and hem you in on every side. They will dash you to the ground, you and the children within your walls. They will not leave one stone on another, because you did not recognize the time of God's coming to you" (Luke 19:37-44).

Countless incidents in the Bible tell of the Lord showing up when He wasn't expected, although He should have been, and showing up in a manner that was surprising. God continues to do this today, and we must be open to the unexpected time and the unexpected manner of His coming. For we may be surprised to find that He has been around and we haven't recognized Him.

"They will dash you to the ground, you and the children within your walls. They will not leave one stone on another, because you did not recognize the time of God's coming to you" (v. 44). Now you couldn't have told anybody in Israel in those days that, if the Messiah came, they wouldn't be ready for Him. The fact is, Israel had been waiting for the Messiah for at least thirteen hundred years.

Moses had said, "The Lord your God will raise up for you a prophet like me" (Deuteronomy 18:15), so they began to look for a prophet like Moses. God had promised David, "I will raise up your offspring to succeed you, who will come from your own body" (2 Samuel 7:12), so they knew He would come through the Davidic line.

But then the prophet Isaiah said, "He grew up before him...like a root out of dry ground. He had no beauty or majesty to attract us to him" (Isaiah 53:2). And the prophet Zechariah warned against despising the "day of small things." It becomes clear that Israel didn't take heed of *all* the messianic prophesies. They were selective. They were so sure of their own picture of the Messiah that they thought, *When the Messiah comes, we'll know Him. Don't tell us we won't know Him.*

Consider for a moment. What if you and I are like Israel? What if we want the Lord to appear, but the way He does it catches us by surprise? Or we are so ill prepared for Him that when He does come, we don't know Him?

Let's look at five examples of the Lord's coming at a surprising time or in a surprising way.

When Obedience Results in a Change of Outlook

God tells Abraham to sacrifice Isaac, and Abraham is ready to obey. He is holding the knife in the air ready to slay his own son, when God says, "Stop! Hold it!"

> "Do not lay a hand on the boy," he said. "Do not do anything to him. Now I know that you fear God, because you have not withheld from me your son, your only son."
>
> Abraham looked up and there in a thicket he saw a ram caught by its horns. He went over and took the ram and sacrificed it as a burnt offering instead of his son. So Abraham called that place The Lord Will Provide (Genesis 22:12-14).

What happened? The Lord appeared in an unexpected way. Hebrews 11:19 says Abraham thought "God could raise the dead," that is, He would bring Isaac back from death. Instead, God just tested Abraham to see if he really would obey.

Abraham's obedience resulted in an unexpected revelation of God that, in turn, increased his trust in God. His way of looking at things was transformed.

When Our Complete Forgiveness of Others
Is Followed by a Time of Blessing by God

Joseph went through a long period of bitterness because of what his brothers had done to him. They had sold him into slavery, and the next thing we know Joseph is working in Egypt as a servant in the house of Potiphar, an Egyptian official. Potiphar's wife tries to seduce him. Joseph rejects her, but she lies and says he tried to rape her. Now he's in prison.

Joseph has every reason to be bitter: first, because of what his brothers did to him; second, because he has been falsely accused. With him in the prison are Pharaoh's butler and baker. Joseph says to the butler, "When you get out in three days remember me

GOD'S TIMING IS PERFECT.

to Pharaoh because I've done nothing wrong to deserve this." But because of this self-pity, which stemmed from his bitterness, God says, "Joseph, you're not ready yet. You need another couple of years here in the dungeon."

We can be sure that, during those two years, Joseph dealt with his bitterness and forgave his brothers (see Genesis 45:1-11) because, unexpectedly, one day the Lord appears. How? There is a knock on the door and a request from none other than Pharaoh for Joseph to come and interpret a dream. The result—Joseph is appointed governor of Egypt. The Lord appeared. When? When the end of his long nightmare coincided with Joseph's complete forgiveness of those who had hurt him, ushering in a time of God's blessing. God knows how much we can bear. His timing is perfect.

When Our Desperation Makes Us Keep On Obeying

The people of Israel have been in bondage for four hundred years. At last Moses arrives, but they're not ready for him, so he goes off to live in the desert. Forty years later he appears again. This time the Israelites clap their hands and say, "It's wonderful! God has sent us the Deliverer!" However, as soon as Moses goes to Pharaoh and says, "Let my people go," things go from bad to worse. Now the Israelites, who are being forced by Egyptian slave drivers to make bricks, have to find their own straw to produce the same number of bricks as before. All the people who were so excited to see Moses turn against him.

Moses says to God, "Lord, you haven't done what you said you would do." What can Moses himself do? He has to keep on obeying. God sends ten plagues, and the breakthrough comes with the tenth—the Passover. The people of Israel, however, have only been traveling three days, getting as far as the Red Sea, when they look up and see Pharaoh's army coming after them! They are terrified and Moses is desperate.

What does the Lord say? "'Why are you crying out to me? Tell the Israelites to move on. Raise your staff and stretch out your hand over the sea to divide the water so that the Israelites can go through the sea on dry ground'" (Exodus 14:15). Moses has to do one more thing, and it isn't praying. It's as though God is saying, "Quit praying and start obeying! Lift up your rod!" So how does the Lord appear? Through Moses' desperation leading him to continued obedience.

Shadrach, Meshach and Abednego refuse to bow down to the golden image that King Nebuchadnezzar has set up (see Daniel 3:1-30). As a result, the king threatens to throw them into the burning fiery furnace. They answer that they don't need to take notice of what he says:

Shadrach, Meshach and Abednego replied to the king, "O Nebuchadnezzar, we do not need to defend ourselves before you in this matter. If we are thrown into the blazing furnace, the God we serve is able to save us from it, and he will rescue us from your hand, O king. But even if he does not, we want you to know, O king, that we will not serve your gods or worship the image of gold you have set up" (Daniel 3:16-18).

Nebuchadnezzar is furious and has the three men thrown into the fire. But then he leaps to his feet in amazement.

> [The king] asked his advisers, "Weren't there three men that we tied up and threw into the fire?"
> They replied, "Certainly, O king."
> He said, "Look! I see four men walking around in the fire, unbound and unharmed, and the fourth looks like a son of the gods" (vv. 24,25).

The Lord appeared when His Hebrew children's crisis led them to continued obedience.

When God Ignores All the Traditional Ways in Which He Has Manifested Himself Before and Appears in an Unprecedented Manner

If someone were to say to you today, "The Lord is going to appear in your life between now and sunset," you would probably say, "Well, if He really is going to appear, I'm sure I'll recognize Him."

Elijah was to see a manifestation of the glory of God unlike anything he had ever seen before (see 1 Kings 19:9-18). It comes at a time in his life when he is depressed, tired and on the run from his enemies. As he shelters in a cave in hiding, God tells Elijah to watch and see what He will do: "'Go out and stand on the mountain in the presence of the Lord, for the Lord is about to pass by'" (v. 11).

First, a great and powerful wind tears the mountains apart and shatters the rocks around him. This has to be the Lord! He has appeared in that way before, as He does later on the Day of Pentecost when the Spirit comes "like the blowing of a violent wind" (Acts 2:2). But we're told that "the Lord was not in the wind." After the wind there is an earthquake. Ah, this must be it! But no—"the Lord was not in the earthquake." After the earthquake comes a fire. Elijah is sure this is the way it should be because God has previously manifested Himself through fire. But "the Lord was not in the fire." After the fire there is "a gentle whisper," what the *King James Version* calls, "a still small voice." "When Elijah heard it, he pulled his cloak over his face and went out and stood at the mouth of the cave" (1 Kings 19:13).

I will never forget when, in 1982, Arthur Blessitt, the man who has carried the Cross around the world, came to Westminster Chapel. People laughed. They said, "He's all right for Hyde Park Corner. But how dare you have a man like that in the pulpit of Westminster Chapel?" I thought, *What if this is God's way of appearing in our midst?* I recognized something authentic in the man. Do you know, he turned us upside down. We have never been the same since. Most of us—in fact, as far as I know, all of us still in the Chapel—thank God he ever came. But it wasn't the way one would expect God to work in a traditional place like this.

The people of Israel were sure they would recognize the Messiah. But Jesus wept over Jerusalem and warned what would happen because they did *not* recognize the time of God's coming.

I daresay that God wants to appear in my life and in yours. The difficulty is that we tell Him how He has to do it. I think a lot of people in Wales today are looking for revival, but are sure that, if revival comes, it's going to be as it was in 1904. Some of us who have seen God work think, *I'll know Him when He comes because I've seen Him before.* The truth is, God may come again and ignore all the traditional ways. He *has* worked through earthquakes. He *has* worked through wind. He *has* worked through fire. But this time He may come in a different manner. Will we recognize Him if He does?

When God Ignores Our Prayer Requests, but Appears with Special Grace Instead

In 2 Corinthians 12:8 the apostle Paul says, "Three times I pleaded with the Lord to take it away from me." To take what away? What Paul calls a "thorn in the flesh." We will never know until we get to heaven what that "thorn in the flesh" was, but it was so awful that Paul prayed for it to go away.

Sometimes we feel discouraged because we have asked God to do something and He hasn't answered. We ask Him a second time, and He doesn't answer. We ask a third time, and He doesn't answer. And we think, *There must be something wrong with me.* Well, what about the apostle Paul? Was there something wrong with him? No. God did answer Paul's prayer, but not in the way he wanted: "'My grace is sufficient for you, for my power is made perfect in weakness'" (v. 9). And Paul's response?

> I will boast all the more gladly about my weaknesses, so that Christ's power may rest on me. That is why, for Christ's sake, I delight in weaknesses, in insults, in hardships, in persecutions, in difficulties. For when I am weak, then I am strong (2 Corinthians 12:9,10).

That was the Lord's way of appearing. Sometimes He ignores our prayer requests, but instead appears with special grace to sustain us.

Years ago my wife and I lived in a little place called Carlisle, Ohio. At the time things were hard. We didn't know how we were going to make it financially with a small, struggling church, people deserting us right and left because they didn't like what I preached, and not enough money for the treasurer to pay my salary! We were down to nothing. I mean, we had nothing. We asked God to send something. Do you know, in the mail that morning, there was a check for $25—a lot of money to us at the time—from a person we hadn't seen in years. He wrote and said, "Yesterday, when I woke up, I felt led to send you $25." If you had told me that was the way God would supply our need, I would have said, "Not from *him*; he doesn't even know where we are!" It's just one of my experiences of God's appearing, but not in the way I thought He would.

So it will be with all of us. That's a promise.

ENTERTAINING AN ANGEL

The Lord appeared to Abraham near the great trees of Mamre while he was sitting at the entrance to his tent in the heat of the day. Abraham looked up and saw three men standing nearby. When he saw them, he hurried from the entrance of his tent to meet them and bowed low to the ground.

He said, "If I have found favor in your eyes, my lord, do not pass your servant by. Let a little water be brought, and then you may all wash your feet and rest under this tree. Let me get you something to eat, so you can be refreshed and then go on your way—now that you have come to your servant."

"Very well," they answered, "do as you say."

So Abraham hurried into the tent to Sarah. "Quick," he said, "get three seahs of fine flour and knead it and bake some bread."

Then he ran to the herd and selected a choice, tender calf and gave it to a servant, who hurried to prepare it. He then brought some curds and milk and the calf that had been prepared, and set these before them. While they ate, he stood near them under a tree.

"Where is your wife Sarah?" they asked him.

"There, in the tent," he said.

Then the Lord said, "I will surely return to you about this time next year, and Sarah your wife will have a son" (Genesis 18:1-10).

The writer of the letter to the Hebrews says, "Do not forget to entertain strangers, for by so doing some people have entertained angels without knowing it" (Hebrews 13:2). Almost certainly this reference goes back to the passage in Genesis where Abraham is gracious to three strangers. They turn out to be angels, and the consequence of Abraham's behavior is that he is promised something he didn't think possible.

Two of the angels who came to Abraham were later entertained by Lot and dramatically rescued him from the destruction of Sodom (see Genesis 19:1-29). Another example of someone entertaining an angel is in the book of Judges, where a man by the name of Manoah and his wife offer hospitality to "a man of God," and God gives them Samson (see Judges 13:1-25).

What are angels? The best definition is given in Hebrews 1:14: "Are not all angels ministering spirits sent to serve those who will inherit salvation?" They are called "spirits" because normally we cannot see them with the naked eye. But if our eyes are opened spiritually—as Elisha's servant's were (see 2 Kings 6:15-17)—then we would probably find that there was an angel at our side at this very moment. At least one!

When we get to heaven, I have no doubt that we will get to see the angel who was sent to be with us from the moment of our birth. Not just from the moment of our conversion, but from the moment of our birth. Because "are not all angels ministering spirits sent to serve *those who will inherit salvation?*" (italics added). Could we not all testify to an awareness of God looking after us before we came to faith?

Because angels are God's servants, they take on any identity that is pleasing to Him. So they may take the form of fire: the burning bush Moses saw was an angel (see Exodus 3:1-6). We are told that the Ten Commandments were delivered through angels (see Acts 7:53; Galatians 3:19). The pillar of cloud by day and the pillar of fire by night that guided the people of Israel in the wilderness could well have been angels (see Exodus 14:19; Numbers 20:16).

Sometimes an angel can look like an ordinary person. The reason the writer to the Hebrews says, "Do not forget to entertain strangers," is that we don't know when we see a stranger whether that stranger is an angel. I think some of us will discover, when we get to heaven, that a particular person we came into contact with was, in fact, an angel.

So, first, angels are God's messengers. Second, they minister to those who are God's own people. You could say they minister to Christians or those who will be Christians. So if you're not saved, but God knows you're going to be saved, an angel is with you now.

Angels are created beings (see Colossians 1:16). All angels have been created by God: they had a beginning. We also know that angels were around during Satan's rebellion in heaven. Peter writes, "God did not spare angels when they sinned" (2 Peter 2:4), and Jude makes reference to angels who did not keep their positions of authority (see Jude 6).

It seems that a certain number of angels lined up with Satan when he rebelled against God. We don't know how many. Some think that in Revelation 12:4 the reference to "a third of the stars" falling from the sky refers to the fall of a third of the angels. We don't know that. Saint Augustine had a theory that the number of God's elect would be equal to the number of fallen angels. Whatever the case, we can be sure that there were angels who did not fall. So the angel that God has sent to be at your side must be an angel who is experienced in spiri-

REMEMBER, THE ANGEL AT YOUR SIDE
IS ONE WHO SAID NO TO SATAN.

tual warfare because he rejected the overture of the devil· You can be sure that when Satan decided to rebel against God in the heaven of heavens, he recruited every angel who would listen to him. The angel at your side is one who said no.

Another thing we know about angels is that they are perfect worshipers of God. There's no way you can divert an angel. There's no way you can flatter him. There's no way you can bribe him and get him to do something for you. How do we know this? Well, we learn in Revelation 19:10 that when an angel appeared to John, he "fell at his feet to worship him." But the angel refused to let John do this, saying, "Do not do it!...Worship God!"

You may think, *I'd love to see my angel.* But if John could fall down to worship an angel, so could you and I, and we would probably be tempted to talk to him instead of to God. The angel is a perfect worshiper of God: He is self-effacing and only does what God tells him to do. So how does an angel minister to us.

Angels Reveal God's Surprising Plan for Us

How do we know that? Well, in the previously quoted extract

from Genesis 18, Abraham is gracious to three strangers and prepares a meal for them. Then, all of a sudden, one of the strangers says, "Where is your wife Sarah?"

"There in the tent," Abraham replies.

The angel says, "I will surely return to you about this time next year, and Sarah your wife will have a son."

What a word! What Abraham has wanted all his life is to have a son. As for Sarah, she can't believe she can have a child at her age.

A similar thing happens in Judges 13:3-5, when Manoah and his wife entertain the man of God. The word comes:

> "You are sterile and childless, but you are going to conceive and have a son. Now see to it that you drink no wine or other fermented drink and that you do not eat anything unclean, because you will conceive and give birth to a son. No razor may be used on his head, because the boy is to be a Nazirite, set apart to God from birth, and he will begin the deliverance of Israel from the hands of the Philistines."

Angels Rescue Us from Our Folly

In Genesis 19, the two angels arrive at Sodom. There they find Lot, where he shouldn't be—Sodom is the most ungodly, wicked spot on the face of the earth. Lot was the kind of man who thought he was strong enough not to give in to temptation. There are those of us who think we prove how strong we are by seeing how close we can get to temptation and rejecting it. But surely the proof that you are strong is not that you get close to temptation and reject it, but that you avoid it altogether if you know it could possibly come along.

Lot was foolish and, as a consequence of living near Sodom, his own sense of morality was compromised. Sodom was a center of homosexual promiscuity, and we are told that all the men in the city wanted to have sex with the two angels.

Lot says, "Look. I cannot allow this. Listen to me, I've got two virgin daughters—let me bring them out to you and you can do what you want with them."

Can you imagine a father saying this about his own daughters? It just shows how Lot had been affected by his closeness to the world. Fortunately, it turns out that those two angels are his salvation, because at the last moment, in the nick of time, they deliver Lot and his family from the destruction of burning sulfur that falls upon Sodom and Gomorrah. According to 2 Peter 2:7-9, the Lord knows how to rescue people from temptation; He knows those who are His. Lot is even referred to as "a righteous man" because he was a saved man.

Angels Comfort Us When We Are in Extreme Depression

Elijah, who seems to have been prone to depression, has just witnessed the greatest victory of his whole ministry. But because of the threat that his enemy, Queen Jezebel, then makes on his life, we find him under the broom tree, praying that he might die (see 1 Kings 19:4). He's feeling sorry for himself. He says, "'I have had enough, Lord,...Take my life; I am no better than my ancestors.'" In his depression, he falls asleep.

When a person is depressed, sometimes all he wants to do is to stay in bed all the time. He just wants to sleep. He can't talk to anybody. When we suffer from depression, we ought to know that God knows we are suffering. He understands. If a man of God like Elijah could know depression, then why should we feel guilty because we do, too?

All at once an angel touched him and said, "Get up and eat." He looked around, and there by his head was a cake of bread baked over hot coals, and a jar of water. He ate and drank and then lay down again. The angel of the Lord came back a second time and touched him and said, "Get up and eat, for the journey is too much for you" (1 Kings 19:5-7).

Angels Guard Us and Protect Us from Trouble

You may wonder why God allows you to have any trouble at all! But what you experience is just a hint of what God *could* let happen. When we get to heaven, we will probably find out how, time and time again, God has rescued us from trouble before it has arrived.

"For he will command his angels concerning you to guard you in all your ways; they will lift you up in their hands, so that you will not strike your foot against a stone" (Psalm 91:11,12).

God sometimes lets us fall just to show us that He's there, actually guiding us, lest we take things for granted. The truth is, however, we will never know until we get to heaven how much trouble has been prevented.

I never will forget my first invitation to Northern Ireland. I was scared to death at the thought of going there. The troubles were at their height. I wrote back and said, "What kind of protection do you give? How do I know I'll get there and back?"

They wrote: "Psalm 34 verse 7—'The angel of the Lord encamps around those who fear him, and he delivers them.'"

Angels Reveal Deep, Hidden Secrets

While I, Daniel, was watching the vision and trying to understand it, there before me stood one who looked like a man. And I heard a man's voice from the Ulai calling, "Gabriel, tell this man the meaning of the vision."

As he came near the place where I was standing, I was terrified and fell prostrate. "Son of man," he said to me, "understand that the vision concerns the time of the end" (Daniel 8:15-17).

We may not understand how, but God uses angels to reveal deep secrets.

It is a mystery why we need angels, why God needs them.

Surely, the Holy Spirit can do everything. But it seems to be part of God's plan and purpose that He created angels mainly for us, "to serve those who will inherit salvation."

Would you like to entertain an angel? Three suggestions:

1. *Be open to anybody at any time.* You never know if God will send someone who will give you a word that is life changing. I have had it happen to me more than once—by being open to just anybody. God spoke, and the person through whom He spoke may, for all I know, have been an angel.

2. *Look in the direction of those who you think could not possibly help you.* Listen to what Jesus said: "'When you give a banquet, invite the poor, the crippled, the lame, the blind, and you will be blessed. Although they cannot repay you, you will be repaid at the resurrection of the righteous'" (Luke 14:13,14). If you want to know how you could possibly entertain an angel, look to people who could not possibly pay you back. God may speak through one of them.

3. *Remember that the angel, or agent that God uses, may be quite nondescript.* He or she may not have wings; there may be no glistening brilliance. You may look at a particular person and think, Well, no angel here. Be careful. You never know!

My friend O. S. Hawkins, who is the pastor of First Baptist Church, Dallas, Texas, once described to me something that happened while he was at his former church in Fort Lauderdale, Florida. One Saturday morning, a man by the name of Bill showed up on their parking lot and asked if he could do a little bit of work in exchange for meals.

Well, they thought, *we'll help him. Though we don't need anybody.* They said, "All right, Bill. Take a broom and sweep."

All day long he did nothing but sweep. He kept talking about this torch that he had bought at the K-Mart, a store nearby—it had cost him five dollars. He was so proud of that red torch. They talked with him a little and they thought, *He's certainly a hard worker.* He went on all day long, never complaining, sweeping every place he could. The next morning, someone thought he saw him in church, though no one was sure; but in the collection bag was the red torch! They never saw him again. O. S. was convinced it was an angel sent to see whether they would be open to just anyone who showed up wanting some kind of help.

Do you want God to appear? What if, by being gracious to someone you didn't think could help you, you got a word that was life changing in return? What an honor! It could happen to you even today.

GOD'S UNRECOGNIZED PRESENCE

Jacob left Beersheba and set out for Haran. When he reached a certain place, he stopped for the night because the sun had set. Taking one of the stones there, he put it under his head and lay down to sleep. He had a dream in which he saw a stairway resting on the earth, with its top reaching to heaven, and the angels of God were ascending and descending on it. There above it stood the Lord, and he said: "I am the Lord, the God of your father Abraham and the God of Isaac. I will give you and your descendants the land on which you are lying. Your descendants will be like the dust of the earth, and you will spread out to the west and to the east, to the north and to the south. All peoples on earth will be blessed through you and your offspring. I am with you and will watch over you wherever you go, and I will bring you back to this land. I will not leave you until I have done what I have promised you."

When Jacob awoke from his sleep, he thought, "Surely the Lord is in this place, and I was not aware of it." He was afraid and said, "How awesome is this place! This is none other than the house of God; this is the gate of heaven" (Genesis 28:10-17).

I think there is a sense in which we can define spirituality as the ability to close the time gap between the moment the Lord appears and our awareness that it is the Lord. Let me put it this way. Perhaps God spoke to you at a particular time or was present on a particular occasion. At the time, it didn't seem as if it was God who was doing the speaking or God who was present at all. What He was doing or what He said you underestimated, if not rejected. Only years later did it become clear to you that you had failed to recognize His presence.

Some of us may take less time to recognize God's presence—weeks or days; others may have it down to only minutes or seconds! So, when our initial feeling is to reject something, we find ourselves thinking instead, *This may be the Lord.*

One definition of spirituality then: the ability to close the gap between the time of the Lord's appearance and our being aware that it is the Lord.

I remember many years ago when Louise and I had moved away from Fort Lauderdale for only eighteen months, we came back and found that something had started called "The Coral Ridge Presbyterian Church." Before we went away, there had been a vacant lot with a big sign on it—"Future home of Coral Ridge Presbyterian Church"—and that sign just stayed there month after month for a couple of years. We wondered, *Whatever is happening here? When will that church start?*

When we came back after the eighteen months away, the church *had* started and it was the talk of Fort Lauderdale. Jim Kennedy, who is the architect of what is now known as

Evangelism Explosion (EE), was using this evangelism method in Fort Lauderdale.

I have to say that I was one of Kennedy's greatest critics. I thought that Evangelism Explosion was not of God. I called it "Arminian," that is, "not God's way." It took two or three years for me to climb down and to see that EE really was of God. But I couldn't see it at the time. I had theological biases; I had other instincts and I went by them.

Perhaps you can think of a similar experience when something came up that at first you thought God simply wasn't in. Then later, like Jacob, you had to say, "The Lord was in this place. I didn't know it. I wasn't aware of it." Let's not think ourselves so spiritual that we are sure we couldn't possibly miss the Lord's presence. Our very biases may keep us from seeing the Lord when He appears.

There are helpful biblical principles. Let's look at Isaiah 53:2 again: "He grew up before him like a tender shoot, and like a root out of dry ground." If we saw a root in a dry piece of ground, we would take no notice of it. We would think, *There's no chance of anything developing from that.* Or again Zechariah 4:10: "'Who despises the day of small things?'" We may find out later that what we thought was a particularly insignificant time was, in fact, very important. God may speak powerfully today and it may only be eighteen months from now that we realize it! What we need to hope for is the ability to recognize the moment when God speaks.

Does God tell us what He's going to do? The answer would have to be—sometimes He does, sometimes He doesn't. But when the Lord does appear, we ought to be able to recognize Him. I would hate to think of the Lord appearing and my not knowing Him. I would love to think that the Holy Spirit within me would recognize the Holy Spirit within someone else; then, if I am where God is at work, I could overrule my biases, my prejudices, my instincts and see that this is God.

Sometimes we are prevented from recognizing God. For instance, when Jesus appeared on the road to Emmaus (see Luke 24:13-35) and the two disciples found a stranger with them, they didn't recognize that it was the Lord because "they were *kept*

ANSWERED PRAYER IS OFTEN STARING US IN

THE FACE, AND WE CAN'T SEE IT.

from recognizing him" (v. 16, italics added). So it may be possible for the Lord to appear and, for some reason, we are kept from seeing Him, and only realize later that He has been in our midst. But often we should have known Him at the time.

Let's reflect on the possibility that God has appeared and we don't see Him, even though we may have been praying for Him to come. He answers our prayer, but we can't believe it, either because our unbelief is too great or because our prejudices overrule our faith. Maybe the Lord appeared yesterday and we didn't realize it. Maybe He has answered prayer and we haven't recognized it.

Here are a few examples of failure to recognize the Lord's presence.

When We Miss What God Is Doing in Another Person
In 1 Samuel 1, a woman called Hannah wanted more than anything in the world to have a baby, but she was barren. She went to the Temple and, in verse 12, we are told:

As she kept on praying to the Lord, Eli observed her

mouth. Hannah was praying in her heart, and her lips were moving but her voice was not heard. Eli thought she was drunk and said to her, "How long will you keep on getting drunk? Get rid of your wine."

Here was a man of God who didn't recognize that the Lord was at work in another person. It may be that you are underestimated by your minister or fellowship group leader. It is quite possible for someone who ministers to you in an official capacity not to realize that God is at work in you.

Dr. Martin Lloyd-Jones, my predecessor at Westminster Chapel, used to tell me the story of Evan Roberts. When Evan was in college and not attending to his studies as he should, many of his tutors were very critical. But one person said, "Don't touch that boy. God is dealing with him." He recognized that the Holy Spirit was at work and, indeed, Evan Roberts turned out to be singularly used in the Welsh Revival of 1904-1905.

On the Day of Pentecost, some people scoffed at the one hundred and twenty believers who were filled with the Spirit and speaking in other languages. They accused them of being drunk (see Acts 2:13). These scoffers could not recognize the hand of the Lord. It should not surprise us that the inability to recognize God at work is often apparent in unbelievers. However, what if God is working in another person and you miss it and, if anything, add to their grief, as Eli the priest must have done when he accused Hannah of being drunk?

When We Miss God's Answer to Our Prayer and Only Later Recognize His Presence

In Acts 12:5 we are told, "Peter was kept in prison, but the church was earnestly praying to God for him." God answered their prayer and freed Peter from jail. Peter went back to the house where they were all gathered and praying.

Peter knocked at the outer entrance, and a servant girl named Rhoda came to answer the door. When she recognized Peter's voice, she was so overjoyed she ran back without opening it and exclaimed, "Peter is at the door!" (Acts 12:13,14).

The very people who had been praying all day said, "You are out of your mind." The very ones who were praying for Peter couldn't believe that God had answered their prayer.

In the passage at the start of this chapter (Genesis 28:10-17), Jacob comes to a "certain place" and stops there for the night. He has a vision of a ladder and angels ascending to and descending from heaven. When Jacob wakes up from his sleep, he thinks, "Surely the Lord is in this place, and I was not aware of it....How awesome is this place!" And he calls the place "Bethel," meaning "house of God." It becomes special because the Lord has appeared there and Jacob comes to see that it really is the Lord.

The background to this story is that Jacob is scared of his brother Esau. Esau has a grudge against Jacob—understandably (see Genesis 27:1-41)—and Jacob is frightened that Esau will kill him. His fear is caused by his external circumstances. Then God answers Jacob's prayer, not by changing the external situation, but by changing Jacob. Something inside makes Jacob see that he is going to live and that God is going to bless him: "Your descendants will be like the dust of the earth" (Genesis 28:14). That proves that he is going to live and not die. The Lord is with him.

Sometimes the way God answers our prayers is not by changing what is around us, but by changing us so that we can cope. Answered prayer is staring us in the face, and we can't see it.

My friend Dr. Michael Eaton, who lives in Nairobi, told me about a group of people who came every week to pray for revival on the second floor of an auditorium, not realizing that down on the ground floor, at the same time, seven hundred Kenyans were coming to pray and worship every week. Revival had already broken out! Those who prayed upstairs were too blinkered to see what God was doing down below!

When We Are Dominated by Fear Even
Though God Is All Around Us

Let's look at the story of Elisha's servant (2 Kings 6:15-17). The servant was terrified: enemy chariots were visible all around them, and he knew they were going to be defeated. The prophet tells him, "Don't be afraid....Those who are with us are more than those who are with them." His servant replies in so many words, "Well, you could have fooled me. There's just you and me, and look at all these against us!"

> And Elisha prayed, "O Lord, open his eyes so he may see." Then the Lord opened the servant's eyes, and he looked and saw the hills full of horses and chariots of fire all around Elisha.

Perhaps you, too, are dominated by fear, when the truth is God is with you. And He's saying to you today, "Those who are with you are more than those who are with them." Jesus said, "'I am with you always, to the very end of the age'" (Matthew 28:20); "'Never will I leave you; never will I forsake you'" (Hebrews 13:5). You may feel that, because of your fear and because of what you see around you, there is no way forward. The truth is God is around you; angels by the dozens, by the thousands, are attending you. Saint Augustine put it this way: "God loves every person as though there were no one else to love."

When We Are Disappointed by the Word God Gives Us

Perhaps you have gone to church or to a Bible study hoping for a word from the Lord, and you have sat there thinking, *Well, so far God hasn't spoken to me. I don't know why I even came.*

Second Kings 5 tells the story of Naaman, who suffered from

leprosy. He hears of the famous prophet, Elisha, through his wife's little Israelite servant girl. She says, "If only my master would see the prophet who is in Samaria! He would cure him of his leprosy" (v. 3). Naaman says, "All right, I'll go." He makes all kinds of arrangements and finally goes to where Elisha is. But Elisha won't even come out to meet him! Naaman feels insulted. Here he is—a commander, an officer—and Elisha won't even greet him. Instead, the prophet sends a message (which Naaman doesn't like at all): "Go, wash yourself seven times in the Jordan, and your flesh will be restored and you will be cleansed" (v. 10).

Naaman goes away angry: "'I thought that he would surely come out to me and stand and call on the name of the Lord his God, wave his hand over the spot and cure me of my leprosy'" (v. 11). "How dare he insult me? Go to the Jordan and wash seven times?!" But,

> Naaman's servants went to him and said, "My father, if the prophet had told you to do some great thing, would you not have done it? How much more, then, when he tells you, 'Wash and be cleansed'!" (v. 13).

Naaman's servants persuade him to believe that this really is a word from the Lord. Naaman goes into the Jordan once and comes out just like he was. The second time—still no change. When he goes in a third time, he thinks, *Well, I'll start getting better now.* But no. Even after the sixth time, there's no difference. But on the seventh time, lo and behold, he is healed completely!

It may be that God *has* given you a word, and you don't like it. You want something else, some other word. Jesus said, "'Whoever can be trusted with very little can also be trusted with much'" (Luke 16:10). Accept what God has given you, and who knows what will happen in the end?

During the Welsh Revival of 1904-1905, a certain young man walked ten miles to meet Evan Roberts. He found out where he was staying and asked to see him. "Well, I'll just see. Just a moment," was the reply.

The person who answered the door went upstairs and said, "Evan, would you see a man who has come to the door?"

Evan said, "No. God won't let me go."

So the messenger had to come back to the waiting young man and say, "I'm sorry. He won't see you."

"Oh, please, I'm distressed. I've got to see him. I've walked ten miles."

Again Evan was asked, "Would you please come and see this young man? He looks very discouraged."

Evan just replied, "No. Tell him 'Psalm 27 verse 10.'"

The messenger went back and said, "I'm sorry. Evan Roberts won't see you. He just told me to tell you, 'Psalm 27 verse 10.'"

The young man, dejected and depressed, went away. But he decided to open his Bible, and he read, "When my father and my mother forsake me, then the Lord will take me up" *(KJV)*. The night before, his parents had thrown him out of the house. It was just the word he needed.

When We Are Blind to What God Is Doing Strategically

Often when we see the way things turn out, our immediate reaction is, God can't be in this. God's Messiah—Isaiah's "root out of dry ground"—ended up hanging on a cross. You know the old spiritual, "Were you there when they crucified my Lord?" I can tell you, if you had been there, you wouldn't have seen anything but a crucifixion. What hint was there that this man on the cross with the blood coming down from His hands, His forehead and His feet was none other than the Son of God dying for the sins of the world? There was no hint at the time that this was God in Christ reconciling the world to Himself.

Looking back at particular times in your life, you might say, "God was at work and I was not aware of it." You may be going through a time of trial at this very moment. James says, "Consider it pure joy,...whenever you face trials of many kinds" (James 1:2). The trial you're going through at the moment may be God's hint that He's there after all.

ON TRIAL
WITHOUT
KNOWING IT

"The King will reply, 'I tell you the truth, whatever you did for one of the least of these brothers of mine, you did for me.'

"Then he will say to those on his left, 'Depart from me, you who are cursed, into the eternal fire prepared for the devil and his angels. For I was hungry and you gave me nothing to eat, I was thirsty and you gave me nothing to drink, I was a stranger and you did not invite me in, I needed clothes and you did not clothe me, I was sick and in prison and you did not look after me.'

"They also will answer, 'Lord, when did we see you hungry or thirsty or a stranger or needing clothes or sick or in prison, and did not help you?'

"He will reply, 'I tell you the truth, whatever you did not do for one of the least of these, you did not do for me.'

"Then they will go away to eternal punishment, but the righteous to eternal life" (Matthew 25:40-46).

"On trial without knowing it." At first glance, this may not seem to be a particularly exciting subject, but the principles that lie behind it might offer you the most gripping insight you have received for a long time. I would like to suggest why.

God Wants to Promote You

God wants to promote you to greater blessing or success or anointing than you have ever known. He is not against your being successful. We can have such a strong reaction against what is known as the "health and wealth" gospel that we go to the other extreme and imagine that God just wants us to be oppressed and suffering all the time. Peter said, "Humble yourselves, therefore, under God's mighty hand, that he may lift you up in due time" (1 Peter 5:6). God doesn't want you to be always under a cloud.

God Promotes Those He Can Trust

God may test us or put us through a time of trial because He wants to see if we get through it with dignity or if we complain all the time. He may say, "Oh, here I was just about to promote that person to a higher level"—but, unfortunately, our own spirit has forfeited the blessing. It is said of Hezekiah, "God left him to test him and to know everything that was in his heart" (2 Chronicles 32:31). It could be that God hides His face from you just to see whether you have reached the stage of being promoted to a higher level of anointing or responsibility. For instance, as we saw earlier, God exalted Joseph to be governor of Egypt because he had at last become someone God could trust.

God Tests Us When We Are Not Aware of It

When God is looking for someone who can be trusted, He may

put us through a test we're not remotely aware is of His design.

A few weeks after Louise and I were married, she got a job working for a lawyer. One day the lawyer came in and asked her, "Where's the money that was lying on the table?" The truth is he had left it out to see what she would do with it.

Louise replied, "Well, I've got it all here. I put it where nobody could see it."

In much the same way, God tests us, when we don't know we're being tested, to see if we can be trusted. We may not know until years later that we were being tested at all. It may be that when we get to heaven and we view a "video replay" of our lives, we will see the times when we were being tested and didn't know it.

Passing the Test Means an Elevation to Glory

If we come through our time of trial faithfully, we will be lifted up and trusted more. God knows He can trust us with greater responsibility: with a more prestigious job, with good health or with a greater income. And He can trust us with a higher level of anointing of the Holy Spirit.

Let's look at some examples of being tested by God without knowing it.

Seeing Jesus and not knowing it. I know of a minister who was invited to spend some time with Mother Teresa. I have never forgotten what she said to him after his first day of working with the poorest of the poor in Calcutta. She had only one question: "Did you see Jesus today?" I often tell our team of street evangelists (we're called Pilot Lights) to treat the very next person God puts in their path with dignity. They are not to look for the person getting out of a Rolls Royce, or for the well-dressed middle-class person, but to take the one who's there. He may be a tramp, he may be a tourist or he may be someone we personally would prefer not to witness to. But we need to treat that person as we would Jesus and give that person attention.

These days, the Church seems to have become almost entirely middle class, and it tends to reach out only to those whom it thinks will make the Church "look good." However, Jesus went to the bottom of the heap. Those who followed Him were not

WHEN WE ARE PUT TO THE TEST UNAWARES,

THEN WE WILL SHOW IF WE REALLY

CAN BE TRUSTED.

perhaps the kind of people we would want to go on holiday with, but Jesus accepted them. He was never ashamed of them. He could say, as it were, "These are My people." This is what God wants of you and me.

Maybe by being eager to be seen with the "right" people, eager to get invited to the "right" events, we are missing entirely what God would do if we simply treated every person we met with dignity. Then one day He could say, as Jesus did, "Whatever you did for one of the least of these brothers of mine, you did for me" (Matthew 25:40), and we will be blessed.

How many times have we seen Jesus and not known it? And how many times will it happen in the future? Will you get to the judgment seat of Christ and have to say, "Lord, when did we see you hungry or thirsty or a stranger or needing clothes or sick or in prison, and did not help you?" He will reply, "I tell you the truth, whatever you did not do for one of the least of these, you did not do for me."

Taking the lowest seat at the banquet. Once, at a meal He was attending, Jesus noticed some of the guests choosing places of honor for themselves (Luke 14:1-14). He told them this parable:

> "When someone invites you to a wedding feast, do not
> take the place of honor, for a person more distinguished
> than you may have been invited. If so, the host who invit-
> ed both of you will come and say to you, 'Give this man
> your seat.' Then, humiliated, you will have to take the
> least important place. But when you are invited, take the
> lowest place, so that when your host comes, he will say to
> you, 'Friend, move up to a better place.' Then you will be
> honored in the presence of all your fellow guests. For
> everyone who exalts himself will be humbled, and he who
> humbles himself will be exalted" (vv. 8-11).

This idea of taking the highest seat at a banquet has more than
one interpretation. For example, you may offer your opinion
when no one asks for it. And by giving it, you find out that no one
wants to know! But if you wait until you're asked, you could be
"exalted." Or you may assume that you are the natural person for
a particular job or promotion at work, and not wait for God to do
the promoting. Here is a salutary tale from the book of Esther:

> When Haman entered, the king asked him, "What should
> be done for the man the king delights to honor?"
> Now Haman thought to himself, "Who is there that the
> king would rather honor than me?" So he answered the
> king, "For the man the king delights to honor, have them
> bring a royal robe the king has worn and a horse the king
> has ridden, one with a royal crest placed on its head. Then
> let the robe and horse be entrusted to one of the king's
> most noble princes. Let them robe the man the king
> delights to honor, and lead him on the horse through the
> city streets, proclaiming before him, 'This is what is done
> for the man the king delights to honor!'"

"Go at once," the king commanded Haman. "Get the robe and the horse and do just as you have suggested for Mordecai the Jew, who sits at the king's gate. Do not neglect anything you have recommended" (Esther 6:6-10).

This was the worst possible scenario Haman could ever have imagined!

But, you see, those who are sure they are the ones next in line are often the ones who are humiliated. Your willingness to be self-effacing, when the temptation is to be the opposite, could be what shows you are ready for glory.

When God seems to appeal to your natural interests. God could be wanting you to do the opposite of what He hints. For example, in Numbers 14, God says to Moses, "You know, these people that are following you are an awful lot. They are a sorry bunch. Do you know what I'm going to do, Moses? I'm going to destroy them all and you and I together will start all over and we'll make a great nation."

In a way Moses must have welcomed that word. It's a word perhaps a lot of deacons might welcome regarding their minister! And I know a lot of ministers who, if God said, "Look, I'm going to get rid of all of your deacons and start all over," would respond, "Wonderful. Thank you, Jesus. Praise God!" But not Moses. When God says to Moses, "I'm going to destroy this lot and make of you a great nation," Moses says, "No, oh no!"

Moses said to the Lord, "Then the Egyptians will hear about it! By your power you brought these people up from among them. And they will tell the inhabitants of this land about it. They have already heard that you, O Lord, are with these people and that you, O Lord, have been seen face to face, that your cloud stays over them, and that you go before them in a pillar of cloud by day and a pillar of fire by night. If you put these people to death all at one time, the nations who have heard this report about you will say, 'The Lord was not able to bring these people into the land he promised them on oath; so he slaughtered them in the desert' (Numbers 14:13-16).

Moses intercedes on behalf of the very ones who had been so stubborn and unkind to him. That's really what God wanted Moses to do. Sometimes God will seem to hand us what our flesh longs for on a silver platter, just to see what we'll do with it. This was Moses' finest hour. He did what God was hoping he would do—he prayed for the people.

"Well," you might say, "that's not fair! How would I know that God really wants me to do the opposite of what seems to be the obvious thing?" It is not obvious, and that is why it is fair. It reveals what we really are. When we are put to the test and not aware of it, when it seems as if we could just name what we want and be granted it, then we will show if we really can be trusted.

When God hides His opinion and asks for yours. "At Gibeon the Lord appeared to Solomon during the night in a dream, and God said, 'Ask for whatever you want me to give you'" (1 Kings 3:5).

I wonder what would happen if God came to you like that. Have you ever fantasized about God saying, "Name it, claim it, you've got it." What would you ask for? What if God sent an angel to you who said, "I have authority to give you anything you want. Just tell me what it is and it's yours." What would you do? You might not think of it as a test, but Solomon, who didn't know he was being tested, asked for the following:

"I am only a little child and do not know how to carry out my duties. So give your servant a discerning heart to govern your people and to distinguish between right and wrong. For who is able to govern this great people of yours?" (vv. 7,9).

In other words, Solomon asked for wisdom.

The Lord was pleased that Solomon had asked for this. So God said to him, "Since you have asked for this and not for long life or wealth for yourself, nor have asked for the death of your enemies but for discernment in administering justice, I will do what you have asked. I will give you a wise and discerning heart, so that there will never have been anyone like you, nor will there ever be. Moreover, I will give you what you have not asked for—both riches and honor—so that in your lifetime you will have no equal among kings" (vv. 10-13).

When we are being tested and God is looking to see what we are really like, if He's pleased with us, He may give us things we didn't even ask for.

When you have just passed one major test and are immediately tested again. I mentioned earlier that when Joseph was working in the house of Potiphar, Potiphar's wife tried to seduce him because he was well built and handsome. Joseph resisted her, saying, "No, it wouldn't be right. I'd be sinning against God and against your husband. No!" And he fled. Then Potiphar's wife accused Joseph of trying to rape her, and Potiphar put him into the dungeon.

Sometimes when we pass a major test—when we don't give in to sexual temptation, or the temptation to take what isn't rightfully ours, or the temptation to lie about or trample all over someone—we feel really good and think, *God must be proud of me.* But then we are surprised to find that on the heels of the first time of testing comes another. Joseph passed the test of Potiphar's wife, but his troubles weren't over!

God said, "Yes, Joseph, you're doing well! But you're not ready to be exalted yet. Your time hasn't come!" God may bring us to the point where we can do nothing but wait for him to work. While we wait we don't realize it, but we're being tested.

Many years ago, I used to sell vacuum cleaners for a living. Do you know, I got into some very important homes. I sold a vacuum cleaner to a multimillionaire Jewish man in Miami Beach who, as it turned out, was the founder of Pepsi-Cola. He had a little black poodle named "Pepsi." The man took a liking to me and I prayed with him once. He wanted me to come back to pray with him again, and I did. I prayed with him a number of times. One day he gave me what at the time seemed to be the greatest honor I had ever experienced. He said, "We're going to have a banquet in the Fontainbleu Hotel"—that is *the* hotel in Miami Beach. He went on, "I want you and your wife to sit at the head table with Joan Crawford"—the famous movie star, who had become chair of the board of Pepsi-Cola—"and me. And I want you to pray at the banquet."

I accepted. Two days before the banquet he called me into his plush home in Miami Beach and said, "Could I just hear a little bit of the prayer you're going to pray?"

I said, "Well, I hadn't thought about it, to be honest."

"Well, could you give me an outline now?"

I said, "Well, all right... 'Our heavenly Father, we thank you for this occasion...'"

He said, "Mm hmm, good, good."

"'Your providence has brought us together for this great evening...'"

"Mm hmm." He liked that!

"'And for raising him up and bringing him from Russia years ago, and for how you've blessed his life. Thank you for all the people here...'"

"Mm hmm. Good."

I went on and on, and then I said, "'We pray these things in Jesus' name. Amen.'"

"Oh... *that!* Do you have to say *that?*"

"Well, yes."

"Now, look here, there'll be a lot of Jewish people here that evening. That will be offensive to them."

I said, "Well, Mr. Darsky, you've heard me pray many times."

"Oh, it doesn't bother me. But it will bother a lot of people there."

I said, "I'm sorry."

"Well," he said, "I'll see what I can do."

But he called me back that evening. He said, "I'm sorry, we'll have to get somebody else." And they got a rabbi to pray.

I think I passed the test. I think God wanted to see what I would do. You see, we're all being tested. You may ask, "Am I being tested? Is God testing me right now?" The answer is, yes!

COPING WITH
TEMPTATION

When tempted, no one should say, "God is tempting me."
For God cannot be tempted by evil, nor does he tempt
anyone; but each one is tempted when, by his own evil
desire, he is dragged away and enticed. Then, after desire
has conceived, it gives birth to sin; and sin, when it is full-
grown, gives birth to death.

Don't be deceived, my dear brothers. Every good and
perfect gift is from above, coming down from the Father
of the heavenly lights, who does not change like shifting
shadows (James 1:13-17).

We have seen so far that God appears in unusual ways, often at
an unexpected time or in an unprecedented manner. What I want
to explore now is how He can even appear through temptation.
Now this is a delicate subject because the Bible says that God
doesn't tempt anybody.

It is said of Jesus that he "was led by the Spirit into the desert to be tempted by the devil" (Matthew 4:1). It seems that, although the devil does the direct tempting, it is the Spirit who may lead us into a place where the devil can do his work.

Or take the example of Job.

Then the Lord said to Satan, "Have you considered my servant Job?" (Job 1:8).

You may know of someone who has been through an enormous amount of suffering. I can think of a friend of mine, Robert Cuffe-Adams, a Christian brother who has known a great deal of pain and trouble. I think when I get to heaven I'll find out that one day God said to Satan, "Have you considered my servant Robert?"

The Bible says, "No temptation has seized you except what is common to man. And God is faithful; he will not let you be tempted beyond what you can bear. But when you are tempted, he will also provide a way out so that you can stand up under it" (1 Corinthians 10:13).

God earmarked Job for greater blessing. He already was greatly blessed, but God wanted to bless him more. You may think, *Well, why didn't God just go on and do it?* I don't know. For reasons I don't understand, God tests us. He tested Job and tested him to the hilt. Maybe He's doing that with you.

Now there are, in fact, two origins of temptation. One is the flesh; the other is the devil. Let's remember, when it comes to the flesh, these words of James: "When tempted, no one should say, 'God is tempting me'" (James 1:13). James says this because, when we are tempted, it often seems as if God is involved. Temptation comes so easily to us. It is so natural, so painless, that even the most mature people may think to themselves, *God is actually in this*, when in fact it is the flesh deceiving us every time.

What about the devil? Paul writes: "I was afraid that in some way the tempter might have tempted you and our efforts might have been useless" (1 Thessalonians 3:5). This shows that we can be tempted directly by the devil. He may use the flesh—indeed, he will. But he also comes alongside and appeals to our intellect; he will work with circumstances; he will put a person in our path who makes us weaker than perhaps another person would. It's amazing how "providential" temptation can appear to be—events come together in a way that seem ordered by God. But Satan has been given certain powers, limited though they are, to cause events to happen or people to come along at just the right moment—or you could say, the wrong moment—and so bring us into temptation. Let's look at some areas of temptation.

Money

There are people whose weakness is simply a love of money, and the devil knows this. Remember that the devil has a "computer printout" of your personality, your background, your weaknesses and your temptations. It is amazing how he can bring things to pass so that, before your eyes, an opportunity appears for you to make money fast, maybe by sailing a little close to the wind. Yet you say to yourself, *Well, this has come my way. And God knows that I need this money.*

Just as Eve in the Garden of Eden saw that the forbidden fruit was "good for food and pleasing to the eye, and also desirable for gaining wisdom" (Genesis 3:6), so you might say, *Well, we need the money.* Over the years I have watched some of my best friends lose their marriages, their homes, their anointings—all because an opportunity to make money fast came along and they took it. If it's legitimate, that's different, but you still have to be very, very careful.

People who want to get rich fall into temptation and a trap and into many foolish and harmful desires that plunge men into ruin and destruction. For the love of money is a root of all kinds of evil. Some people, eager for money, have wandered from the faith and pierced themselves with many griefs (1 Timothy 6:9,10).

WHEN YOU ARE FAITHFUL TO GOD,
HE WILL OVERRULE THE OBSTACLES
THAT STAND IN YOUR WAY.

The person who gives in to the love of money will be giving in to his or her weakness. Judas Iscariot had an inherent weakness for money:

Then Mary took about a pint of pure nard, an expensive perfume; she poured it on Jesus' feet and wiped his feet with her hair. And the house was filled with the fragrance of the perfume.

But one of his disciples, Judas Iscariot, who was later to betray him, objected, "Why wasn't this perfume sold and the money given to the poor? It was worth a year's wages." He did not say this because he cared about the poor but because he was a thief; as keeper of the money bag, he used to help himself to what was put into it (John 12:3-6).

We read in Mark 14:10,11: "Then Judas Iscariot, one of the Twelve, went to the chief priests to betray Jesus to them. They were delighted to hear this and promised to give him money. So he watched for an opportunity to hand him over." Who would have thought that the person who walked with Jesus for three years would, at the end of the day, betray him for thirty pieces of silver?

Jesus said, "Whoever can be trusted with very little can also be trusted with much, and whoever is dishonest with very little will also be dishonest with much" (Luke 16:10). So the person who helps him- or herself to just a few coins from the till would also rob a bank of a million dollars if given the opportunity.

Ananias and Sapphira were professing Christians (see Acts 5:1-11). The Holy Spirit gave many in the Early Church such a detachment from the love of material things that they sold their property and laid the money at the apostles' feet. Ananias and Sapphira claimed to have done exactly this, but they gave in to the love of money. They kept some back. God honored what the church was doing, so Peter could say to Ananias, "How is it that Satan has so filled your heart that you have lied to the Holy Spirit and have kept for yourself some of the money you received for the land?" (Acts 5:3). The result was that Ananias and then Sapphira were struck dead by the Spirit.

The ability to handle money is God given. Most of us don't have it. This is why God keeps the opportunity to make a lot of money from us. We couldn't cope with it.

Sex

Sooner or later every Christian must pass this test. We are tested to see if we can be trusted to be faithful to the principles of Scripture when it comes to morality. Sex outside marriage is not part of God's plan, and it is only a matter of time before those who give in to it will be sorry.

We see stories on the front pages of newspapers almost every day of prominent people who have been tripped up by sexual temptation. Billy Graham said not long ago to a friend of mine, "It seems that the devil gets seventy-five percent of God's best men through sexual temptation." Whether they're in politics or religion, the public wants its leaders to be clean and moral. If you're a Christian, God wants the same of you.

Let's look back again at Joseph and his run-in with Potiphar's wife. God had earmarked Joseph for a special task: "One day I'm going to make that man governor of Egypt." But Joseph was tempted by Potiphar's wife. It was the perfect opportunity for an affair: Joseph was away from home, away from his father, away from his brothers—nobody back in Canaan would ever know. You can be sure Potiphar's wife didn't want her husband to know! However, Joseph said, "I couldn't do this. It wouldn't be right for my master and I would be sinning against God."

You can tell what you are when the opportunity for the perfect affair emerges, and you think, *Well, this time there is no way I could get caught.* The funny thing is Joseph was punished because he did not have an affair. But it was a test. God knew the truth and God exalted him. Humanly speaking, Joseph didn't have a chance; but when you are faithful to God, He will overrule the obstacles that are in your way.

Samson was also earmarked for a special task, but he had a weakness for women and all these women he was involved with gave him trouble (see Judges 14:1—15:6; 16:1-3). His final downfall was brought about by Delilah, who bullied him into telling her the secret of his great strength—his hair. Samson gave in to Delilah because she kept nagging him—"You never confide in me. You don't really love me"—until, we're told, "he was tired to death" (Judges 16:15,16). Then Delilah betrayed him to his enemies.

> When Delilah saw that he had told her everything, she sent word to the rulers of the Philistines, "Come back once more; he has told me everything." So the rulers of the Philistines returned with the silver in their hands (v. 18).

Samson suffered because of his weakness for women, and how sorry he was!

Sadly, some people are tested even at the height of their careers when it would seem they have gone as far as they can go. King David had conquered Jerusalem and had brought the Ark of the Covenant to the city. He was on top of the world. Then one day he walked out on his balcony and saw a young woman who was bathing (see 2 Samuel 11:2-4). He said, "I've got to have her. Who is she?" The word came back: "Well, first of all, she's married. Second, her husband is one of your soldiers." He said, "Bring her to me." However, what David thought would be the perfect afternoon affair came to tragedy when Bathsheba became pregnant (v. 5). David said, "No problem," and had her husband, Uriah, killed. He hoped no one would know (vv. 6-26). But God knew.

Unsanctified Ambition

Ambition is the desire to achieve, and it's a God-given thing. *Unsanctified* ambition is a desire to achieve that which has not been brought under the control of the Holy Spirit. It causes us to set our sights on a particular position—we say, "I've got to have that." James and John may have been guilty of unsanctified ambition when they put this request to Jesus:

> Then James and John, the sons of Zebedee, came to him. "Teacher," they said, "we want you to do for us whatever we ask."
>
> "What do you want me to do for you?" he asked.
>
> They replied, "Let one of us sit at your right and the other at your left in your glory."
>
> "You don't know what you are asking," Jesus said. "Can you drink the cup I drink or be baptized with the baptism I am baptized with?"
>
> "We can," they answered (Mark 10:35-39).

But they were wrong. They thought they were ready, but they were not. This is why Jesus said, "I have much more to say to you, more than you can now bear" (John 16:12). And he could say to us, "I've got many things I'd like you to do, but you're not ready yet."

If we're not careful, unsanctified ambition will cause us to set our sights on getting that important job, that prestigious position or that invitation, or on being seen with the right people. We may become so consumed with ambition that God in heaven—who may have earmarked us for a special mission—looks down and says, "Oh, I wish he hadn't done that" or "if only she hadn't wanted to be seen with that person or hadn't bragged about herself in that way."

Other Temptations

Another area of temptation is unbelief. Unbelief is the origin of fear, and the devil used fear to tempt Jesus: "If you are the Son of God, tell these stones to become bread" (Matthew 4:3). He was trying to get Jesus to doubt who He really was.

Again, in the Garden of Eden, the devil said to Eve, "Did God really say, 'You must not eat from any tree in the garden'?" implying that perhaps God hadn't (Genesis 3:1). Unbelief diverts us from our real calling and from seeing the truth of God's Word.

Another temptation is to be bitter and unable to forgive. There are many who just can't forgive people who have hurt them. Perhaps the degree to which we cannot forgive someone else will be the degree to which we block our own blessing from God. God may not trust us with a greater anointing or promote us to a higher level of blessing. Hebrews 12:15 says, "See to it that no one misses the grace of God and that no bitter root grows up to cause trouble and defile many."

Joseph, who overcame sexual temptation and was eventually given grace to forgive his brothers, was exalted to a high place because he could be trusted. The reason for the dearth of greatness on the horizon today is because small men and women live to get even. God may be looking high and low for one person who can be trusted with honor because he or she can forgive.

Other areas of temptation are losing your temper or speaking about someone in a manner that will cause others not to think very highly of that person anymore. Remember, Jesus said, "'But I tell you that men will have to give account on the day of judgment for every careless word they have spoken'" (Matthew 12:36). Another temptation is to seize an opportunity to exalt or promote yourself. I think of the words of an old spiritual:

He sees all you do, He hears all you say, My Lord
is writing all the time.

Resisting Temptation
What might help us resist temptation? Three suggestions:

1. Remember that temptation is a test from God, and that any temptation is resistible (see 1 Corinthians 10:13).
2. Imagine how you're going to feel if you don't give in to it, and how you're going to feel if you do.
3. Remember that God is looking for those He can trust.

ENFORCED LEARNING

And you have forgotten that word of encouragement that
addresses you as sons:

"My son, do not make light of the Lord's discipline, and
do not lose heart when he rebukes you, because the Lord
disciplines those he loves, and he punishes everyone he
accepts as a son."

Endure hardship as discipline; God is treating you as
sons. For what son is not disciplined by his father? If you
are not disciplined (and everyone undergoes discipline),
then you are illegitimate children and not true sons.
Moreover, we have all had human fathers who disciplined
us and we respected them for it. How much more should
we submit to the Father of our spirits and live! Our fathers
disciplined us for a little while as they thought best; but
God disciplines us for our good, that we may share in his

holiness. No discipline seems pleasant at the time, but painful. Later on, however, it produces a harvest of righteousness and peace for those who have been trained by it (Hebrews 12:5-11).

> When through the deep waters I call thee to go,
> The rivers of woe shall not overflow.
> For I will be with you, your troubles to bless,
> And sanctify to you your deepest distress.
> —Hymn in Rippon's SELECTION 1787

Many years ago, in the summer of 1956, I collapsed on my grandmother's bed—I was in her home   and said, "Lord, why?"

Twelve months earlier, I had been on top of the world. I was pastor of my first church   my father's pride and joy. Never before had there been a preacher in the family. My grandmother was so proud of me that she bought me a brand-new car. Then something happened. I had what you might call "a Damascus road experience"—I came to know the Lord for Himself. It changed my theology; it changed my whole outlook.

Several months later, however, my father became disappointed in me, and my grandmother even took the car back! And then, with my friends and relatives pointing the finger at me and rolling their eyes heavenward, I lay on that bed, saying, "Lord, why?" I was not prepared for this, but it was the Lord's way of appearing to me.

Now this doesn't happen to me every day, but at that point a verse came into my mind, Hebrews 12:6. I thought, *Whatever is this? I'll look it up and see.* I read: "For whom the Lord loveth he chasteneth, and scourgeth every son whom he receiveth" *(KJV)*. This was my introduction to a subject that may best be described as "enforced learning," because, you know, God has His own way of teaching us things we wouldn't normally want to learn.

There are two ways of looking at this subject of enforced learning or chastening or disciplining. One way is to see it as punishment; the other is to see it as preparation or training. If you see it as punishment, then you may think of it as God getting even with you. I remember a lady coming to my study some years ago and saying, "I know why this has happened to me. It's because of something I did many years ago."

I said, "That's nonsense. God is not getting even with you. Don't you know that He got even at the cross when He punished His Son for our sins?"

As the psalmist says, "As far as the east is from the west, so far has he removed our transgressions from us" (Psalm 103:12).

Well, then, you ask, *if God doesn't chasten us to get even with us, why does He do it?*

I would say that He does it not to punish us, but to prepare us. Just as any father disciplines his son, so our heavenly Father knows exactly what we need, because He isn't finished with us yet. Being prepared is essentially being trained, and that's the word used in the passage at the beginning of this chapter. "No discipline seems pleasant at the time, but painful. Later on, however, it produces a harvest of righteousness and peace for those who have been *trained* by it" (italics added). There are a number of things we need to understand.

Enforced Learning Is Inevitable If You Are a Christian

Notice how the writer puts it: "The Lord disciplines those he *loves,* and he punishes everyone he *accepts* as a son. Endure hardship as discipline; God is treating you as sons. For what son is not disciplined by his father?" (Hebrews 12:6,7, italics added).

There are those who say they don't sin. They really don't think they're sinners, either because their theology is faulty or because they lack objectivity about themselves. If you ever run into a Christian who claims not to sin, ask this question, "Does God ever chasten you?"

If he or she says yes, then ask, "Well, would He have to if you weren't a sinner?"

If the person says, "No, God never chastens me," he's just told you he's not a Christian. If you *are* a Christian, what the writer is describing here will inevitably happen to you sooner or later: "The Lord disciplines those he loves." If God *doesn't* correct you when you are living in disobedience, you need to ask why. It is an ominous sign to be devoid of God's chastening. It suggests that He is not dealing with you at all, and that is a bad position to be in!

CHASTENING IS NOT THE MOST DESIRABLE WAY TO HAVE GOD APPEAR, BUT IT CAN BE THE MOST MEMORABLE—AND THE MOST TREASURED.

Perhaps I should say at this point that there are three kinds of chastening. I think of them as internal, external and terminal chastening.

Internal chastening is when God speaks to you directly through His Word. I call it "internal" because it happens in your heart. The Bible says that the Word of God is "sharper than any double-edged sword" (Hebrews 4:12), and when God operates, say, through preaching, it hurts. Internal chastening is the best way to have God deal with you. It's secret. You may feel exposed, you may feel everybody can see what's happening, but they can't. It's between you and God.

If God deals with you this way, thank Him for it, because the second kind of chastening, *external* chastening, is far less preferable. If God speaks to you through a word that's preached or a prophetic word or a word of knowledge, or through a friend gently trying to make a suggestion, and you reject that message, then you leave Him no choice but to do what He has to do to get your attention. He's done it with me, and believe me, external chastening is no fun.

The third kind of chastening, which I won't dwell on too long, is *terminal* chastening. There are two sorts of terminal chastening.

One is when God just takes you home to heaven, as happened in 1 Corinthians 11 to those who abused the Lord's Supper. The apostle Paul says, "For anyone who eats and drinks without recognizing the body of the Lord eats and drinks judgment on himself. That is why many among you are weak and sick, and a number of you have fallen asleep" (vv. 29,30). Those members of the Corinthian church didn't listen to God, and God just took them home to glory. They're saved, but they'll be saved by fire.

Then there are those whom God allows to live for a while, but never to hear Him speak again. They are like King Saul, who said, "'God has turned away from me. He no longer answers me, either by prophets or by dreams'" (1 Samuel 28:15). Hebrews 6:4-6 describes this second sort of terminal chastening.

Enforced Learning Is Painful

Chastening is not the most desirable way to have God appear, but it is probably the most memorable and it can be the most treasured. Our parents made mistakes when they disciplined us, and those of us who are parents make mistakes with our children. But when God disciplines us, He does it perfectly. Whereas we parents may think partly of our own reputation and what will be thought of us if we don't discipline, God thinks only of *us*. He "disciplines us for our good, that we may share in his holiness" (Hebrews 12:10).

"No discipline seems pleasant at the time, but painful" (v. 11). The writer to the Hebrews is addressing discouraged Jewish Christians, and he's actually having to say to them that one of the reasons they are discouraged is that they have forgotten this exhortation: "Do not make light of the Lord's discipline, and do not lose heart when he rebukes you" (v. 5).

You may think, *Well, why say that to someone who's already discouraged?* Perhaps you are in a situation where you are confused and depressed; nothing is like it was and there seems to be no rhyme nor reason why you're going through what you are. However, if you stop and think, *This is God,* how much easier it is to live with! Just consider what pains God is going to to get your attention! For, as the writer says to these discouraged Christians, "This discipline is a sign that God loves you and that he has a work for you to do."

Enforced Learning Is One of God's
Ways of Getting Our Attention

How do we know this? Well, it may be that He hides His face, or appears to betray us. It could be that He withholds a vindication. Have you ever taken a stand no one agrees with, and longed for God to show everyone you're right? But God withholds His vindication to chasten you. Or God may chasten you through financial disaster; or a reversal of good health, when suddenly you're flat on your back and you can't see how long it will be before you recover. It may be through not getting that job you wanted, or that pay raise. It may be by having to work with the one person in the office you can't stand. It may be the loss of a friend. However it comes, it is God's "thorn in the flesh" for you. He has many ways of chastening us.

Don't despair. The wonderful thing about chastening is that there's a purpose in it. It is "for our good, that we may share in his holiness."

Enforced Learning Is God's Way of Preparing Us

Charles Spurgeon said, "If I knew I had twenty-five years left to live, I would spend twenty of them in preparation."

Most of us don't like preparation. We want to get on with things. There is a certain kind of preparation that we all need, however, though we may not think we need it at first. I have been pastor of Westminster Chapel now for many years. When I came here, I was forty-one years old, I had pastored other churches and I had been to theological college and Oxford University. I thought, *At long last, I'm ready to preach. I'm ready to move on.* Little did I know that I was about to begin the greatest period of preparation I have ever known. God's been dealing with me ever since.

We will never know when, out of the blue, God will have to chasten us. It's not pleasant, it's not fun, it's not the way we hope He'll appear; but the day will come when we look back on a dark hour, as I do on that August afternoon in 1956, and say, "Thank you Lord." It's wonderful to know that He chastens us because He loves us and that He appears like this because He has a plan, because we are chosen for something. We may not be ready for it yet, but we will be.

ENCOUNTERING THE DEVIL

Finally, be strong in the Lord and in his mighty power. Put on the full armor of God so that you can take your stand against the devil's schemes. For our struggle is not against flesh and blood, but against the rulers, against the authorities, against the powers of this dark world and against the spiritual forces of evil in the heavenly realms. Therefore put on the full armor of God, so that when the day of evil comes, you may be able to stand your ground, and after you have done everything, to stand. Stand firm then, with the belt of truth buckled around your waist, with the breastplate of righteousness in place, and with your feet fitted with the readiness that comes from the gospel of peace. In addition to all this, take up the shield of faith, with which you can extinguish all the flaming arrows of the evil one. Take the helmet of salvation and the sword of the Spirit, which is the word of God. And pray in the Spirit on all occasions with all kinds of prayers and requests. With this in mind, be alert and always keep on praying for all the saints (Ephesians 6:10-18).

Whatever does encountering the devil have to do with waiting for God to appear?

Donald Gray Barnhouse used to say, "While we wait, we can worship." I would like to say, "While we wait, the devil will turn up." We pray in the Lord's Prayer, "Lead us not into temptation, but deliver us from evil" or, as it is in the Greek, "the evil one." Nonetheless, if the devil should appear, it may be proof that God is at work! It may, in fact, be a word of encouragement to us.

How do we know it is God at work when Satan appears? There are three reasons.

Satan Always Works Within God's Perimeters

Satan has scope to work only to the degree given him by God. Every time he attacks or tempts, he has been given permission from God to do so.

Then the Lord said to Satan, "Have you considered my servant Job? There is no one on earth like him; he is blameless and upright, a man who fears God and shuns evil."

"Does Job fear God for nothing?" Satan replied.

The Lord said to Satan, "Very well, then, everything he has is in your hands, but on the man himself do not lay a finger" (Job 1:8,9,12).

So today God might say, "Have you considered my servant Robert?" "My servant Jim?" "My servant Louise?" When you know the devil is attacking you, just remember, God okayed it before it happened.

Satan Always Attacks When He Is Threatened

In Revelation 12:10-12 we read of the account of those who overcame "by the blood of the Lamb and by the word of their testimony; they did not love their lives so much as to shrink from death." However, the passage continues, "But woe to the earth and the sea, because the devil has gone down to you! He is filled with fury, because he knows that his time is short."

The eighteenth century American theologian, Jonathan Edwards, once said, "Never forget that Satan was trained in the heaven of heavens." I wonder if you have ever noticed—again quoting Jonathan Edwards—that "Whenever the church is revived, so is the devil." Why did Jesus meet so many demon-possessed people? Did His appearance cause people to be demon possessed? Surely not. But, when Jesus appeared, the devil was threatened and Satan always attacks when he is threatened. If you are under attack right now, don't despair—it's a good sign! It's a sign that you're special to God, and that you're a threat to the devil. You must be doing something right!

AS FAR AS SATAN KNEW,
THE CRUCIFIXION OF JESUS WAS HIS IDEA.
BUT IT TURNED OUT TO BE GOD'S WAY
OF SAVING THE WORLD!

Satan Always Becomes God's Unwitting Instrument to Promote the Kingdom of God

The devil always overreaches himself. The verb "overreach" means to be too ambitious, to go too far and then to be sorry. The irony is that the devil never learns! You would think by now he would see that every time he attacks he overreaches himself and only ends up advancing the very purpose he tried to threaten.

The classic proof of this can be found in the crucifixion of Christ. We could say that the devil was, in a sense, the architect of what took place on Good Friday. "The evening meal was being served, and the devil had already prompted Judas Iscariot, son of Simon, to betray Jesus" (John 13:2). The crucifixion of Jesus, as far as he knew, was his idea. When he pulled off the crucifixion of the Son of God, he must have thought that it was the cleverest thing he had ever done. However, it turned out to be God's way of saving the world! The best-kept secret from the foundation of the world was why Jesus would die on a cross. First Corinthians 2:8 says, "None of the rulers of this age understood it, for if they had, they would not have crucified the Lord of glory."

Ananias and Sapphira were both prompted by Satan to lie to the Holy Spirit (see Acts 5:1-11). Both were struck dead instantly. Our reaction might be, *How horrible! Surely such a thing would stop the growth of the church.* Sometimes, today, we think that if something weird happens in a service it will put visitors off and they will never come back.

Last year at our School of Theology, when we were dealing with spiritual warfare, we had the strangest satanic attacks I have known in years. I wasn't surprised, but we all thought, *Oh dear, no one's going to want to come back if they see this sort of thing happening in a place like Westminster Chapel.*

Well, what do you suppose happened when Ananias and Sapphira were struck dead? "Great fear seized the whole church and all who heard about these events" (v. 11). "Nevertheless, more and more men and women believed in the Lord and were added to their number" (v. 14). The devil overreached himself.

In Acts 6:1-7, the Grecian Jews complained about the Hebraic Jews because the Greek widows were being overlooked in the daily distribution of food. The devil was trying to get in, trying to divide the church. What was the result? The apostles chose seven men to minister as deacons in the church. After this happened, we are told, "So the word of God spread. The number of disciples in Jerusalem increased rapidly, and a large number of priests became obedient to the faith" (v. 7).

Satan always becomes God's unwitting instrument to promote the kingdom of God because he overreaches himself.

How does Satan appear? Basically, in two ways. He may come as an angel of light, or he may come as a roaring lion.

An angel of light. "Satan himself masquerades as an angel of light" (2 Corinthians 11:14). He comes in a very subtle manner, he comes quietly and plausibly, and he comes to discredit the truth.

1. Satan is a liar and the father of liars (see John 8:44). Therefore, even if he's telling the truth, you should keep him at bay. In the words of William Perkins, the great Puritan, "Don't believe the devil, even when he tells the truth."

2. Satan comes to distort the Word in disguise. He may use a minister; he may use a church leader; he may use someone you were sure was a man of God. Have a look at the way he came to Eve (see Genesis 3:1). He deceived her by misquoting God ever so slightly. There are people who pose as ministers and when they speak, you think, *Well, I heard I should be wary of this person but what he said seemed plausible.* They distort the truth ever so slightly. The serpent said to the woman, "Did God really say, 'You must not eat from any tree in the garden'?" (Genesis 3:1). The truth is God didn't say that at all (see Genesis 2:16,17).

3. Satan tries to get us to doubt—"Did God really say...?"— so that we are perplexed, not knowing what to believe. Or as the devil said to Jesus when he tempted Him, "*If* you are the Son of God" (Matthew 4:3, italics added). As if Jesus might not be, trying to get Him to doubt.

4. Satan quotes the Bible for his own end. When he was
   tempting Jesus, the devil quoted from Psalm 91:11,12: "He
   says he will give his angels charge over you." Never forget that the devil knows the Bible back to front. Don't
   be surprised if he puts a verse in your mind that seems
   to justify what you are about to do when, in fact, it's
   wrong.

5. The devil comes to tempt. In 2 Corinthians 2:11, Paul
   says, "We are not unaware of his [Satan's] schemes."
   And in 1 Thessalonians 3:5, he is called "the tempter."

A roaring lion. The devil may also come noisily, terrifyingly:
"Your enemy the devil prowls around like a roaring lion looking
for someone to devour" (1 Peter 5:8). Do you know why a lion
roars in the jungle? It is to intimidate its prey. If the devil comes
in noisily, you are intimidated, and you think, *Well, there's
nothing to do but to give in.*

When the devil comes in as a roaring lion, it will be to upset
you, to quench the Spirit within you, to get you to say things that
are unguarded and that you are going to regret, to get you to lose
your temper or overstate your case. When these things happen,
the devil makes you think, *Well, it's too late, I'm defeated.* He
tries to intimidate you and to devour you. But remember, we
often think we have been devoured when, in fact, we have only
heard the lion's roar, and the devil hasn't got us after all.

What can we do to avoid succumbing to the devil? There are
five things, and they all begin with *R*. The five *R*'s of spiritual
warfare: Remember, be Ready, Recognize, Refuse and Resist.

- *Remember* that the devil is round about us. When things
  seem at their quietest, he may be just around the corner.
- Be *ready*. He comes when we don't expect him.
- *Recognize* him for who he is. This requires discernment, of course, and I would say that if one definition

of spirituality is the ability to close the time gap between the Lord's appearing and our recognition that it is indeed He, another would be the same ability to recognize the arrival of the devil.

- *Refuse* him. Don't listen to him. Don't dignify his suggestion by even considering it.
- *Resist.* Twice in the New Testament, in James 4:7 and 1 Peter 5:8,9, we are told to resist the devil. All we need to know is that the devil is resistible. He is powerful, he is the prince of this world, but, as John says, "the one who is in you is greater than the one who is in the world" (1 John 4:4).

THE UNEXPECTED DISRUPTION

Now Moses was tending the flock of Jethro his father-in-law, the priest of Midian, and he led the flock to the far side of the desert and came to Horeb, the mountain of God. There the angel of the Lord appeared to him in flames of fire from within a bush. Moses saw that though the bush was on fire it did not burn up. So Moses thought, "I will go over and see this strange sight—why the bush does not burn up."

When the Lord saw that he had gone over to look, God called to him from within the bush, "Moses! Moses!"

And Moses said, "Here I am."

"Do not come any closer," God said. "Take off your sandals, for the place where you are standing is holy ground." Then he said, "I am the God of your father, the God of Abraham, the God of Isaac and the God of Jacob." At this,

Moses hid his face, because he was afraid to look at God.

The Lord said, "I have indeed seen the misery of my people in Egypt. I have heard them crying out because of their slave drivers, and I am concerned about their suffering. So I have come down to rescue them from the hand of the Egyptians...So now, go. I am sending you to Pharaoh to bring my people the Israelites out of Egypt" (Exodus 3:1-10).

Everything is going well. You're feeling on top of the world, sailing leisurely along with the wind at your back, comfortable, secure and happy. Then everything changes. All of a sudden, without notice, something awful happens and nothing is ever the same again.

One day many years ago, in 1952, when I was sixteen years old, I was sitting at our table in Ashland, Kentucky, with my father, my mother and my little sister who was just one year old. I remember it so well. My dad said, "I believe I'm the happiest man in the world. I've got a home, a wife, a son, a daughter, a job, a church—I cannot imagine being happier." Just one year later he buried his wife, my mother, and came home to hear my grandmother, who had been looking after my little sister, say, "I can't cope anymore." Dad had to manage somehow. To this day, he has never forgotten that moment when he said, "I'm the happiest man in the world."

Why do catastrophes like this happen? I would have to say, because God allows them to happen. It may not seem right, it may not seem fair, but when something goes wrong, it reminds us that this life is not all there is. A friend of mine said to me recently, in all honesty, "Do you know, I hear of people who have suffered. I've never known suffering." But I also know people who, it seems, have never known anything but suffering. I can only imagine that those who undergo suffering are earmarked for a special reward in heaven.

I can't be sure of all the reasons God allows a great disruption to change everything. However, it certainly means preparation for heaven above and preparation for usefulness here below. When you go through tribulation, it means that God is not finished with you yet. It could be that there's something wonderful around the corner.

The Disruption of Conversion

A man by the name of Saul of Tarsus was on his way to Damascus. He wasn't going to hear Billy Graham; he wasn't going to an evangelistic campaign; he wasn't going to a prayer group. He was going to arrest Christians for being Christians. As for himself, the thought that he needed to be converted was laughable and unthinkable. Here was a man who had everything: "circumcised on the eighth day, of the people of Israel, of the tribe of Benjamin, a Hebrew of Hebrews; in regard to the law, a Pharisee; as for zeal, persecuting the church; as for legalistic righteousness, faultless" (Philippians 3:5,6). Saul was, in his own way, doing everything that he thought was right.

Then, out of the blue, something happened that disrupted his life forever: "suddenly a light from heaven flashed around him. He fell to the ground and heard a voice say to him, 'Saul, Saul, why do you persecute me?'" (Acts 9:3-5). How did he respond? He asked, "'Who are you, Lord?'" (He didn't know what he was saying!) The reply was, "'I am Jesus, whom you are persecuting.'" For Saul it was the beginning of a new era.

Have you experienced the great disruption that conversion brings? In the preface to his *Commentary on the Psalms*, John Calvin refers to a "sudden conversion, an unexpected conversion." People have wondered what he meant. In fact, all conversions are sudden; all conversions are unexpected. You may think, *I've been brought up as a Christian.* Well, you may have been taught about Christian things, but there's no guarantee that such teaching has converted you. Do you know what a Christian is? A Christian is a person who is *surprised* that he or she is a

Christian. If you don't stand back in amazement that you have been converted, you probably haven't been converted at all.

The Life-Changing Disruption

God causes another kind of disruption, which we read about in the passage at the beginning of this chapter. Moses has been living in the desert and there's every reason to believe that these forty years were among the happiest of his life. God has given him a wife; God has given him security. He is a family man who has little responsibility.

One day Moses gets up as usual, and notices a bush on fire at the foot of the mountain. At first, he probably doesn't think much of it, but, as he looks again and again, he notices that this particular bush just keeps burning. What's more, though the bush is burning, it isn't being consumed by the flames. Moses' curiosity is aroused. He goes over to the bush, and what happens? He has an encounter with God that changes his life. God says, "I'm sending you to Pharaoh to bring my people, the Israelites, out of Egypt." Moses wants to argue with God, and he says, "Who am I? I'm a nobody." But he was called.

WHAT IF GOD WERE TO DISRUPT YOUR LIFE
AND SAY, "THIS IS WHAT I WANT OF YOU"?

How would you respond? Maybe you have a good job, security and money coming in. And you get a tap on the shoulder. At first you shrug it off. You think, *There's nothing in this.* But, before you know it, God has said, "I want you to do something for me." What if He were to call you to full-time ministry? What if He were to call you to be a missionary? Would you say, "Me? Who am I?"

Do you know one of the saddest things about the ministry today? George Bernard Shaw said, "Those who can, do; those who can't, teach." But I sometimes think, Those who can't, *preach*. There are people going into the ministry today who are mediocre and ordinary and ungifted. It was different three hundred years ago. Then the best men went into the ministry. Today, the best men and women may be lawyers or doctors or nuclear physicists or computer scientists. You may be high powered yourself. What if God were to disrupt your life and say, "This is what I want of you"?

Moses shouldn't have been surprised at God's calling, because we're told that Moses, when he had grown up, refused to be known as the son of Pharaoh's daughter. He chose to be ill-treated along with the people of God rather then to enjoy the pleasures of sin for a short time (see Hebrews 11:24,25). The truth is, when Moses left the palace of Pharaoh, he wasn't planning to turn back. But to prove himself to his fellow Hebrews, to show he was on their side, he killed an Egyptian. He jumped the gun. The word got out, and he had to lie low for a while before God was ready to use him. Then came that sudden great moment when God said, "This is what I want you to do."

Let me tell you something that happened to me. I have a little Bible that I often carry with me, and I had it with me in 1970 when my wife, Louise, and I were at the Southern Baptist Convention in Denver, Colorado. For a number of days the Holy Spirit had been dealing with me. At the time, I was pastor of a church in Fort Lauderdale, Florida. I had a thirty-minute broadcast on the radio every week, and was on television regularly. I had security and we were happy. Then I began to have this uneasy feeling that God was saying, "I want you to go to seminary."

I thought, *What do I want to go to seminary for? What could I learn? I can preach now. I know the Bible.*

But God said, "You need to go."

I thought, *Lord, at my age? By the time I finish all my education I'll be forty years old!*

We were seated high up in the gallery in a church in Denver. And I thought my heart was going to pound out of my chest. I said, "Lord, is this really *you* talking to me? Do you realize I'll be forty years old by the time I finish? I'm going to have to give up this security, and for what? What do I need seminary training for when I already know the gospel? What can they teach me?" I said, "I've got this little Bible here. If you're really speaking to me, let me open it at a verse that will confirm that this is from you!" I wanted something specific. I *didn't* want a verse that just said, "Thus saith the Lord, 'I am with you.'"

My wife was listening to the sermon and was unaware of what was going on. I took the Bible and said, "Lord, you open it for me." (I've got it marked with the date, June 3, 1970.) My eyes fell on these words, "And Moses was learned in all the wisdom of the Egyptians, and was mighty in words and in deeds. And when he was full forty years old, it came into his heart to visit his brethren the children of Israel" (Acts 7:22,23, *KJV*). I nudged Louise. I said, "We're going to have to give up everything." It was *the* disruption. We have never been the same since. I have never doubted, either, that it was God.

God has a way of disrupting our lives. It could be through conversion. It could be by calling us to give up what we have. It could be through financial difficulties. It could be that someone very close to you will be ill and you will have to care for that person, or somebody around you will have a nervous breakdown and you will be affected by it.

Can I ask you this question? What kind of faith would you have if a great disruption came and your life was never the same again? Would you panic? Would you say, "God, how could you let this happen to me"? Or is it possible that you would be like Job who refused to question God or to charge him with foolishness, saying, "Though he slay me, yet will I hope in him" (Job 13:15)?

When God Hides His Face

Rejoice in the Lord always. I will say it again: Rejoice! Let your gentleness be evident to all. The Lord is near. Do not be anxious about anything, but in everything, by prayer and petition, with thanksgiving, present your requests to God. And the peace of God, which transcends all understanding, will guard your hearts and your minds in Christ Jesus.

Finally, brothers, whatever is true, whatever is noble, whatever is right, whatever is pure, whatever is lovely, whatever is admirable—if anything is excellent or praiseworthy—think about such things. Whatever you have learned or received or heard from me, or seen in me—put it into practice. And the God of peace will be with you.

I rejoice greatly in the Lord that at last you have renewed your concern for me. Indeed, you have been concerned, but you had no opportunity to show it! I am not saying this because I am in need, for I have learned to be content whatever the circumstances. I know what it is to be in need, and I know what it is to have plenty. I have learned the secret of being content in any and every situation, whether well fed or hungry, whether living in plenty or in want. I can do everything through him who gives me strength (Philippians 4:4-13).

I wish it were true that, when we are close to the Lord—feeling His presence, hearing His voice, knowing that He is at hand—He would take the time to say, "Oh, by the way, next Tuesday afternoon about a quarter past three, you'll notice that I'll be withdrawing the light of my countenance from you. I'll be hiding My face from you from that time onward for a while."

Sooner or later, we all discover that—without notice, without warning, without the slightest hint that it's going to happen—God hides His face. "Truly you are a God who hides himself, O God and Savior of Israel" (Isaiah 45:15).

As new Christians, we discover it and sometimes the enormity of it is almost too much. As mature Christians, we rediscover it. Or we may have been away from the Lord for a while, have come back and renewed our vows, and somehow feel God is going to make our way smooth from now on. But, as restored people, we, too, find that we must go through times when God's face is hidden from us. We may have been obedient, we may have felt the Lord very near; but without any warning, without any provocation, without anything causing it that we can put our finger on, suddenly He is gone. He's not there, and it's awful.

You may recall the words I quoted from 2 Chronicles 32:31 about King Hezekiah: "God left him to test him and to know everything that was in his heart." God withdrawing His presence is probably the fundamental ingredient in chastening, which we looked at in chapter 7. "The Lord disciplines those he loves, and

he punishes everyone he accepts as a son" (Hebrews 12:6). John
Newton wrote:

> How tedious and tasteless the hours
> When Jesus no longer I see;
> Sweet prospects, sweet birds and sweet flowers
> Have all lost their sweetness to me.

I have often said, perhaps hastily, that I think I could endure
anything as long as I sensed the "light of his countenance," the
"smile" of God's face. Were He to withdraw the light of His face
from me, I could not go on.

In Numbers 6:24-26 we read the blessing Moses gave to Israel:
"'The Lord bless you and keep you; the Lord make his face shine
upon you and be gracious to you; the Lord turn his face toward
you and give you peace.'"

And in Psalm 16:6 we read: "The boundary lines have fallen for
me in pleasant places; surely I have a delightful inheritance." God
is being very good to us when He smiles. So what does it mean
when we say "God hides His face"? I define it as "feeling deserted by God." The "smile" of God's face is feeling Him near and
being conscious of His approval. When He has hidden His face,
you may feel He's angry with you or, worse, that He's betraying
you.

Breaking the Betrayal Barrier

Perhaps the most important accomplishment in the history of
the human race is what I call "breaking the betrayal barrier." This
is something we all have the opportunity to do every time God
hides His face from us. But breaking that barrier is something, I
fear, very few of us manage.

When God hides His face and we feel betrayed—when it
seems the very One we have tried to affirm has turned against us
and is not keeping His word or not doing what He promised,

when we feel that the bottom has dropped out of our world—our immediate reaction is, "God, how could you do this to me?" My experience as a pastor is that ten out of ten Christians sooner or later feel betrayed by God. Yet only one out of ten breaks the "betrayal barrier." Nine out of ten feel so let down and angry that they say, *Well, if that's the way God is going to treat me, after all that I've suffered for Him, then I just don't think I like God anymore—I'm not going to serve Him.*

Is that "chip on the shoulder" attitude going to impress Him? The Bible says, "man's anger does not bring about the righteous life that God desires" (James 1:20). So if we're feeling sorry for ourselves, God may, in fact, delay in delivering us from the trouble we're in.

CHUCK COLSON SAID, "GOD NEVER PROMISES TO TAKE US OUT OF THE FIRE, BUT HE DOES PROMISE TO GET INTO THE FIRE WITH US."

However, one out of ten, I reckon, breaks the betrayal barrier. This is the challenge for us. Can we break that barrier? Those who do are made of the same stuff as the people of faith listed in Hebrews 11, who did things in their generation that were so remarkable that the writer of Hebrews says, "The world was not worthy of them" (v. 38). Rare people indeed, the few who graduate with honors in the University of the Holy Spirit. Like Shadrach, Meshach and Abednego who found that, when they were thrown into the fiery furnace, a Fourth Man was in the fire with them. Chuck Colson put it like this: "God never promises to take us out of the fire, but He does promise to get into the fire with us."

Breaking the Barrier of the Popular Gospel

The fact that God may hide His face does not enter into the "popular gospel" that is often preached today. The popular gospel today is the "health and wealth gospel," the "name it and claim it," "believe it and receive it" gospel, which I mentioned briefly earlier. There are those who say that, if you're really obeying God, you're going to be blessed, you're going to be healed, you're going to have money!

You may think, *Well, what about the apostle Paul who had a thorn in his flesh?* Do you know what one American preacher had to say about that? He said—and I'm not making this up—"If the apostle Paul had had my faith, he wouldn't have had his thorn in the flesh!"

What does Paul actually say? He says, "I know what it is to be in need, and I know what it is to have plenty. I have learned the secret of being content in any and every situation, whether well fed or hungry, whether living in plenty or in want. I can do everything through him who gives me strength" (Philippians 4:12,13). You see, it is no sign that you are spiritual if you say, "Praise God!" when everything is going well for you. The proof that you are spiritual is that, when the bottom falls out of your world and you feel betrayed and deserted, you can say like Job— and mean it—"Though he slay me, yet will I hope in him" (Job 13:15). And you find yourself breaking the betrayal barrier.

So it is no sign of great grace, then, to serve God when everything is going well. If everything does go well, what good is that? You will never know how strong you are until you have been tested. Passing a test is a sign of strength and, as we have seen, the essence of a test is feeling deserted.

The hiding of God's face is always ill timed. It never happens at the moment when you feel ready to cope with anything. It happens when you're in a situation where you don't think you can cope for another day. If you're in despair, consider Jesus. In His worst moment of testing, when they were taunting Him, saying, "Hey, Son of God, come down from the cross!" He could pray, "Father, forgive them, for they know not what they do." Yet while He was praying for more and more grace, He suddenly cried out, "My God, my God, why have you deserted me?"

The Reward for Endurance

The reward is tremendous for the one who doesn't give up. Sir Winston Churchill could say in Britain's finest hour, "We will never, never, never give up." How strong, then, may be the resolution of the Christian who has Jesus Christ with him or her, the One who promised that he would never leave us nor forsake us (see Matthew 28:20)!

Are you waiting for God to appear? Are you ready for God to appear if the way He does it is by hiding His face? For when God hides His face, He is appearing. He doesn't do it accidentally. He doesn't do it because He's having an off moment. He does it on purpose. The truth is, God never really hides His face; He only appears to. Behind the clouds, the sun is always shining.

Coping When God Hides His Face

How we cope when God hides His face will make a difference. If we cope well, it will change us internally and change things around us, even though at the time we may feel deserted and will not be conscious of God's presence or know what He's up to.

When Martin Luther stood before the Church hierarchy at the Diet (or Council) of Worms in April 1521 and said, "Here I stand, I can do no other, God help me, Amen," these were not triumphant words as far as he was concerned. Do you know the story? Luther had been brought in before the Diet and was asked, "Dr. Luther, are these your tracts?" They were spread out on a table before them.

Luther looked at the tracts and he said, "Yes, they are mine."

"Dr. Luther, will you recant what you have written in these tracts?"

Luther asked for twenty-four hours to think about it and they agreed to his request.

That night, in his cell, Martin Luther walked back and forth, crying out to God in the kind of desperation that makes you think, *How unfair of God to treat Luther like this!* If you were God, the Architect of the Great Reformation, wouldn't you have sent a thousand angels into Luther's cell to comfort him and say, "We're for you up here in heaven"?

Instead, Luther has to cry out, "My God, are you dead? No, You cannot die, You only hide Yourself."

The next day, Luther appeared before the church hierarchy again, and they said, "Dr. Luther, are these your tracts?"

He said, "Yes."

"Dr. Luther, will you recant what you have written in these tracts?"

He said, "I do—if you can prove they are contrary to the Word of God. But if not, here I stand, I can do no other, God help me, Amen."

Luther felt very lonely, yet he broke the betrayal barrier, and the world was never the same again.

Will you break the betrayal barrier? You don't have to be a genius. The most ordinary person can do the most extraordinary thing there is, and that is to experience the hiding of God's face and never, never, never give up. It could be your finest hour.

LETTING GOD LOVE US

We know that we live in him and he in us, because he has given us of his Spirit. And we have seen and testify that the Father has sent his Son to be the Savior of the world. If anyone acknowledges that Jesus is the Son of God, God lives in him and he in God. And so we know and rely on the love God has for us.

God is love. Whoever lives in love lives in God, and God in him. In this way, love is made complete among us so that we will have confidence on the day of judgment, because in this world we are like him. There is no fear in love. But perfect love drives out fear, because fear has to do with punishment. The one who fears is not made perfect in love (1 John 4:13-18).

It is my opinion, having been a pastor for many years, that the hardest thing in the world to believe is that God really loves us. It is harder to believe that than to believe that there is a God or that Jesus died on the cross or even that He rose from the dead. It's not too difficult to believe that God will take care of you, or that "in all things God works for the good of those who love him" (though we may not believe that they are for our good at the time!). We can be detached from life sufficiently to look back and say yes, it all worked out. No, the hardest thing in the world to believe is that God, the true God, really loves us, right now, just as we are.

Are you ready for God to love you? It's easy to say, "I certainly am"; but are you really ready to accept and affirm His love?

Why Should We Let God Love Us?

Because He does. We are loved with "an everlasting love" (Jeremiah 31:3). We know that we are loved by Jesus Himself: "'A new command I give you: Love one another. As I have loved you, so you must love one another'" (John 13:34).

There is an even more dazzling truth, and that is that God loves you as much as He loves Jesus. Have you any idea how much God loves Jesus? Have you any idea how God feels about His one and only Son? The voice that came from heaven at Jesus' baptism said, "You are my Son, whom I love; with you I am well pleased" (Mark 1:11). The voice that came at the Mount of Transfiguration said, "This is my Son, whom I love. Listen to him!" (9:7).

What possibility could there be that Jesus could lose His place in the Trinity, that Jesus could be dislodged from the Godhead? Yet Romans 8:17 says, "We are...co-heirs with Christ." That means God loves us as much as He loves Jesus. In John 17:23, Jesus actually prayed that we would see that God loves us as much as He Himself is loved: "'May they be brought to complete unity to let the world know that you sent me and have loved them even as you have loved me.'"

Because God wants us to enjoy His love for us. If I love some-one, but he or she doesn't feel it, then I am unfulfilled. I want the others to *know* that I love them. A mother wants her child to feel her love. How much more does our heavenly Father want us to feel His love!

Because God chose us. He chose us before we were born (see Romans 9:11), yet He knows what we are like. Jesus could say to Nathaniel, "'I saw you while you were still under the fig tree before Philip called you'" (John 1:48). As Gerald Coates has put it: "God does not get disillusioned with us, because he never had any illusions in the first place!"

I don't understand the rationale behind God's choosing me; I only know that it is not based upon works (see 2 Timothy 1:9). Those God loves He has already chosen, and when we let God love us, we dignify His choice of us, however unworthy we feel. He wants us to know how deeply He cares and to affirm this.

Because of God's grace. His grace and His plans take into account our failures, unbelief, self-righteousness and fear. The sacrifice of Calvary assures us that our sins are washed away by the blood Jesus shed on the cross. Therefore, we may know that whatever impediment, fault, failure or defect that haunts us, the blood of Jesus washes it away. The demonstration of God's love is, "while we were still sinners, Christ died for us." He didn't die for us because He saw we were going to turn out all right. He didn't die for us because we had already come up to standard. He died for us when we were utterly unworthy.

Furthermore, God has His own secret way of dealing with us, at our pace and His. The things that are wrong in me He will deal with in His time. He may deal with a fault someone else has in a different way at a different time. We must not judge one another, knowing that God will eventually deal with each of us.

Because He is God. We should let God love us because we so desperately need the kind of love that only God can give. "God is love."

Believing God's Love

First John 4:16 is a verse you could read a thousand times and yet not fully grasp. The *King James Version* says, "And we have known and believed the love that God hath to us." It's easy to read that and not take it in. The *NIV* makes it a little clearer: "And so we know and rely on the love God has for us." I wonder if you have reached the stage where you just rely on God's love for you? You don't rely on *your* love for Him, because you know that goes up and down all the time. Note the following words from the familiar hymn "Come Thou Fount of Every Blessing":

> Prone to wander, Lord, I feel it,
> Prone to leave the God I love.

"The heart is deceitful above all things and beyond cure. Who can understand it?" (Jeremiah 17:9). You cannot rely very long on your love for God. But can you rely on His love for you? He wants you to. Just think how much it would thrill Him if you really believed He loves you. Because most people don't. When we get to heaven, we'll find out how much God loved us on this earth, and many of us will bow our heads in shame. If we could only grasp this life-changing truth, that God really does love us, what a wonderful feeling it would be.

Why are we so loath to believe that God loves us? There are five possibilities:

1. We may have an overly scrupulous conscience, to use the Puritan phrase, and worry about every little thing that may be wrong in our lives.
2. We may still be living under the Old Covenant, under the Law, in the way of many of the Puritans. It's no great surprise to discover that a number of the great Puritan preachers weren't sure they were saved at the time of their deaths.

3. We may have a faulty theology. What we believe theologically is all-important—a warped theology will certainly affect our outlook.

4. There could be a psychological problem. I know people who can't call God "Father" because of the relationship they had with their own fathers. It may surprise you to know, I sympathize here. I never quite came up to my own father's expectations. No matter how well I did, he would say, "Son, you can do better." I remember crying all the way home from school because I had a *B* on my report card—the rest were *A*'s. I knew what Dad would say and, sure enough, he said, "Well, pretty good, son. Next time you can have all *A*'s if you really work." You may have a similar feeling that you can never come up to standard.

5. When we are aware of how much we have failed God (and we have all sinned and let Him down), we can't believe that He still loves us. He wants to love us as we are, and we should not respond to His love by "performing" for Him. (see Isaiah 29:13). When we pretend to be "nice," to love God and be God-centered, we are actually focusing on ourselves and being self-centered. We are guilty of hypocrisy and of being manipulative, trying to "bribe" God to be on our side. It's as if we are saying, "See how good I am, Lord. Now will you love me?" This is obnoxious to God, although He knows why we do it. However, this attitude will not allow Him to love us as we are. We may think, *Well, He shouldn't.* God says, "But I do!" And 1 John 1:9 says, "If we confess our sins, he is faithful and just and will forgive us our sins and purify us from all unrighteousness."

If you can identify with one or all these criteria, at the end of the day, you can still claim the promise that God loves you. But I sympathize. I find it difficult to believe God loves me. For this reason, a few years ago, I began doing something at the beginning of the day when I spent time alone with the Lord to pray. I still do it now. I refer to two Scripture references: Hebrews 4:16 and 1 John 4:16. The first says, "Let us then approach the throne of grace with confidence, so that we may receive mercy and find grace to help us in our time of need." The second, 1 John 4:16, is the verse we read earlier: "And so we know and rely on the love God has for us." So every day I'm aware that I'm asking for mercy, but I'm believing in His love. I have come to see that it really is true: God loves me. God loves you. God really does love us.

When I have to battle against unbelief, I refuse to accept any other option but to rely on His love. I believe it. Any other thought will come from the devil who doesn't want us to believe that God loves us, who will accuse us and call to our attention every sin we have committed in the past to cast us down. The devil doesn't want you to believe that God loves you, but God loves you very much and He loves you just as you are.

We have all had bad moments when we feel unworthy. I want to tell you what I do at my lowest moments. If I'm ever at rock bottom (and I wouldn't want you to know how often that is), I remember that Jesus died for me, because I know that's true. The reason I know it's true is that He died for us all. I feel sorry for the people who believe in limited atonement—the view that Jesus only died for the elect—because, when you are discouraged and you're looking for some hope that God loves you, you're in real trouble if you believe that teaching!

I hang on to those verses that say He died for everybody. In fact, Martin Luther went so far as to say he was glad that John 3:16 didn't say, "God so loved Martin Luther, that if Martin Luther believed he would not perish but have everlasting life." When asked, "Why?" he replied, "Because I would be afraid it referred to another Martin Luther."

But John 3:16 says "'For God so loved the world that he gave his one and only Son, that whoever believes in him shall not perish but have eternal life.'"

So when I'm aware of all that I've done that's wrong and I feel awful, I just plead the merit of Jesus' blood as though I had never been converted. Then I ask for mercy: "God be merciful to me, a sinner."

SOMETIMES MY HEART CONDEMNS ME,

BUT GOD IS GREATER THAN MY HEART.

"Let us then approach the throne of grace with confidence, so that we may receive mercy and find grace to help us in our time of need" (Hebrews 4:16). This verse was addressed to Christians, and we are still asking for mercy. You never outgrow asking for mercy.

So if my heart condemns me, and sometimes it does, I hold on to the truth that God is greater than my heart (see 1 John 3:20,21).

Affirming God's Love

God wants us to affirm His love when we are depressed. You see, if you can affirm His love for you when you're depressed, then that shows you really do believe in it, and that pleases Him. It doesn't take a lot of faith to affirm His love for you when you're on top of the world. But if you're down at the bottom and you can say, "I know you love me," God is pleased.

We must affirm God's love when we have sinned, even though we admit we have given Him enough reason to sever our relationship. We need to say, "Lord, I know I don't deserve it, but I know You love me."

We must affirm God's love when we are happy. The wonderful thing about God in His love for us is that He is the one person we can share our happiness with. Romans 12:15 says, "Rejoice with those who rejoice; mourn with those who mourn." It's far easier to find somebody who will weep with you than to find somebody who will rejoice with you. But you can share everything with God. He's not jealous of your victory, your success or your good news.

Let God love you through friends and people who will accept you. A friend is someone who knows all about you and still loves you! Accept the friend who wants to help you. Let that friend love you and restore you in the spirit of gentleness, in case he or she too is tempted (see Galatians 6:1).

My own experience is that God has a way of drawing near to me when I feel at my most unlovable. All of a sudden, I sense His presence, and I'm amazed. I think, *Lord, You can't do this. Of all the times for You to manifest Your love to me!* God loves to do that. When you are feeling at your most unworthy and least deserving—I don't know why—He'll just love you.

You feel the way the disciples felt on the evening of that first day of the week after Jesus' crucifixion, as they hid themselves away, terrified of reprisals from the Jewish authorities. They had denied Jesus, fleeing from Him when He most needed them. Now He's risen from the dead, and He walks through a locked door, saying, "'Peace be with you!'" (John 20:19). Jesus could even say to Simon Peter, "'You will disown me three times. Do not let your hearts be troubled. Trust in God; trust also in me'" (13:38—14:1). You see, God just keeps on loving us. Loving us with an everlasting love.

ACCEPTING
GOD'S CALL

When they had finished eating, Jesus said to Simon Peter,
"Simon son of John, do you truly love me more than
these?"

"Yes, Lord," he said, "you know that I love you."

Jesus said, "Feed my lambs."

Again Jesus said, "Simon son of John, do you truly love
me?"

He answered, "Yes, Lord, you know that I love you."

Jesus said, "Take care of my sheep."

The third time he said to him, "Simon son of John, do
you love me?"

Peter was hurt because Jesus asked him the third time,
"Do you love me?" He said, "Lord, you know all things;
you know that I love you."

Jesus said, "Feed my sheep. I tell you the truth, when

you were younger you dressed yourself and went where you wanted; but when you are old you will stretch out your hands, and someone else will dress you and lead you where you do not want to go." Jesus said this to indicate the kind of death by which Peter would glorify God....

Peter turned and saw that the disciple whom Jesus loved was following them,...he asked, "Lord, what about him?"

Jesus answered, "If I want him to remain alive until I return, what is that to you? You must follow me" (John 21:15-22).

Our God is a God who calls people. This fact is essential to His dealings with us. After they had sinned, Adam and Eve "heard the sound of the Lord God as he was walking in the garden in the cool of the day,...the Lord God called to the man, 'Where are you?'" (Genesis 3:8,9). Could it be that God is seeking you? The sound of His voice is disquieting, and you may think, *Oh no, it couldn't be that He's calling me.*

What Is God's Call?

Let me define what I mean by God's call: I mean God getting our attention to make His wish known. For example, He calls at conversion. Everyone who is a Christian is a Christian because he or she has been converted, and the reason for the conversion is that the person heard the call of God.

You could say that God's calling comes in two stages. You might like to imagine a circle, and another circle inside it. The big circle is God's general call and the smaller one is His specific call. The Bible says, "For many are called [the large circle of people], but few are chosen [the inner circle]" (Matthew 22:14, *KJV*). What's the difference? Well, the "many" who are called are those who hear preaching. The "few [who] are chosen" are those who hear the specific call. Reformed theologians would regard this as the "effectual call," when God breaks through the barriers and gets to our heart of hearts and wins us over.

What is the difference between the general call and the specific call? Well, the general call is when your natural ear hears something. The specific call is when your spiritual ear hears the voice of the Lord. The general call, when it starts out, is just a voice; but at some stage, if God breaks through, you find yourself saying, "Uh-oh, this means me," and it becomes the specific call. You find that what you are hearing isn't a human voice at all; it's God's voice, and He has penetrated the layers of hardness, of coldness, of defensiveness, and He got through to you. "Few are chosen." It is a wonderful thing when you hear His voice.

Paul wrote to the church at Rome, "You...are among those who are called to belong to Jesus Christ" (Romans 1:6) "And those he predestined, he also called; those he called, he also justified; those he justified, he also glorified" (8:30). He wrote to the Corinthians, "Brothers, think of what you were when you were called. Not many of you were wise by human standards; not many were influential; not many were of noble birth. But God chose the foolish things of the world" (1 Corinthians 1:26,27). The earliest church wasn't the middle-class phenomenon that the Church, at least in the West, is today. Most of the members of the Early Church were at the bottom of the socioeconomic system.

Are we ready for God to select ordinary people? As I said earlier, one of the things I have tried to teach in my own church in London is that we must never be selective in our evangelism. God is indiscriminate. Jesus took people as they were; that's the way God's calling is. Are we willing for God to be Himself, and are we willing to accept those whom He has called?

The Call to Conversion
Before we can be saved we have to be called. This begins with the general calling, but there may be a specific call that lets you know God is on your case. The Bible says, "Seek the Lord while

he may be found; call on him while he is near" (Isaiah 55:6). Maybe you have said, "One day I will call on God." But there comes a time when the Lord just appears, and that's the moment you had better grab because you may never have the chance again.

IF THE LORD HAS COME, IF HE IS NEAR,
YOU MUST SEIZE THE MOMENT.

God says, "My Spirit will not contend with man forever" (Genesis 6:3). Don't think for a minute that the way you feel now is the way you will feel a week from now. If the Lord has come, if He is near, you must seize the moment. This is the time He may be found. Two weeks from now, two years from now, you might not have the slightest concern about God. You could lose your own soul.

"The ground of a certain rich man produced a good crop. He thought to himself, 'What shall I do? I have no place to store my crops.'

"Then he said, 'This is what I'll do. I will tear down my barns and build bigger ones, and there I will store all my grain and my goods. And I'll say to myself, "You have plenty of good things laid up for many years. Take life easy; eat, drink and be merry."'

"But God said to him, 'You fool! This very night your life will be demanded from you. Then who will get what you have prepared for yourself?'" (Luke 12:16-20).

Life goes on, and you think it will always be like this. It may end, however, without notice.

A Special Calling

There is a calling that comes at a deeper level. After conversion, there is what you might call a "special calling" or a "vocation." What is God's will for your life? One day, unexpectedly, God made it clear to me that I was to preach. I come from a part of the hills of Kentucky where those who were called to preach often had spectacular calls. A friend I grew up with heard an audible voice saying, "Dale, preach!" Someone else was plowing corn in the fields when he saw the clouds were formed in a *PC*. He said, "God is saying to me 'Preach Christ,'" and he quit plowing corn and he started preaching Christ. (Those who heard him very often said that the *PC* really meant "Plow Corn"!)

A Deeper Calling

I used the example of a circle within a circle, but dare I think of an even smaller circle within that one, where you get to the very center of God's will, perhaps at great cost? Could it be that there is a call to a spirituality at a deeper level than you have known? What if, in your midlife, when things are going well, God puts his finger on your lifestyle, the way you have been spending your time, your money—all the comfort you have taken for granted—and says, "I have something else in mind." The pain can be great, but the reward will be greater.

I have referred already to our Pilot Light ministry on Saturdays and to the time we invited Arthur Blessitt to preach at Westminster Chapel. The two things are linked. When Arthur came, I didn't think for a moment it would have any particular effect on me.

I didn't dream it would change my life. I had come to the church in 1977, having spent three years at Oxford doing a doctorate in theology. My thesis was published by Oxford University Press, which was a great honor. And do you know what my aspiration was? I can tell you now, though I wouldn't have admitted it then. I wanted to be a world-class theologian.

Then Arthur Blessitt came to us and got us out on the streets. I had never done anything like that in my life! It's one thing to stand up in the pulpit and preach (it is far easier to preach to a hundred than it is to one!), quite another to go up to a total stranger. I could see what God was doing. Things were closing in on me, and it hurt! I could see all that I wanted in terms of my aspirations, but God said, "I've got another idea." I had to become a fool in the eyes of many people, but I was never the same again.

Without notice, God may step into your life, and say, "You've lived as you pleased long enough." God has a right to do that because, "You are not your own; you were bought at a price" (1 Corinthians 6:19,20). He has the prerogative to say at any time, "I want you."

Jesus says to Peter, "Peter, do you love me?"

"Yes, Lord."

"Peter, do you love me?"

"Yes, Lord."

"Peter, do you love me?"

Peter says, "What do I have to say to tell you? Yes, Lord, I love you."

And Jesus announces plans for Peter that show his life will not be like it has been. He even tells him how he is going to die. Then, as soon as Jesus has told Peter what he wants him to do, Peter sees John and says, "What about him?" And Jesus' response? "It's none of your business."

God may single you out and you may think, *Why me? What about him?* It hurts all the more if God makes you do something He doesn't make another person do. But our God is unpredictable in the way He calls us. He may call you through something that's negative—a crisis in your marriage or in a friendship. He may call you through an unusual kind of suffering. He may call you at church or at home. You may be watching television! Suddenly God burdens your heart. In a very short period of time

God can so deal with you that, before you know it, your life is changed. You may look back and see how your life can be divided between "before" and "after" that moment.

The "calling of God" is "getting our attention to make His wish known." Are you ready for this? If not, get ready, for it is only a matter of time—God will call you.

THE
PROPHETIC
WORD

Now we ask you, brothers, to respect those who work hard among you, who are over you in the Lord and who admonish you. Hold them in the highest regard in love because of their work. Live in peace with each other. And we urge you, brothers, warn those who are idle, encourage the timid, help the weak, be patient with everyone. Make sure that nobody pays back wrong for wrong, but always try to be kind to each other and to everyone else.

Be joyful always; pray continually; give thanks in all circumstances, for this is God's will for you in Christ Jesus.

Do not put out the Spirit's fire; do not treat prophecies with contempt. Test everything. Hold on to the good. Avoid every kind of evil (1 Thessalonians 5:12-22).

"Do not treat prophecies with contempt." Do you know, quite unexpectedly, God may send a person into your life with a word that will change everything.

Jeannie's Story

Two or three years ago a lot happened in one evening for which I was not prepared. One Friday night, a woman—her name is Jeannie Raborg—came to my wife and said she wanted to speak to her. Louise politely agreed, although it would mean missing the baptismal service that was about to start. Jeannie's word to her was more or less as follows:

> I was born in Arizona, in a nominal Presbyterian home. I'm not sure if my parents were really Christians. But I can remember they sent me to a girls' youth camp when I was eight years old. On the last evening we gathered around the bonfire and the leader said, "Girls, throw your pine cone into the fire and make a wish." I said, "God, if you're really there, I'd like to know you." That was my wish. Years later I went away to university and met my husband. We were happily married. But when I was about forty years old and teaching school, a student brought a question up to my desk. The next thing I remember was that I was in hospital. They had to send for my husband. I'd had a nervous breakdown. Things went from bad to worse until he had to put me in a secure hospital. The iron door closed on me and I cried, "Please don't put me here!" My husband wept and said, "I don't know what else to do."
>
> Four years after that, an evangelist came to our town, and my mother went to hear him. When he offered healing prayer, she went forward, saying, "I'm not here for myself. I'm here for my daughter who is in a mental institution. Would you pray for her?" He did, but before the

evening was over the Lord spoke to that evangelist and said, "I want you to go to that woman's hospital."

I won't go into how the evangelist had to do that, except to say that he phoned the next day and spoke to a little girl, the granddaughter of the woman who had come forward for prayer, Jeannie's daughter. He asked her for the name of the hospital her mother was in and she couldn't give it to him. He found out eventually, but before she hung up the phone, he said to the little girl, "Tell your grandmother and your father that your mother will be home in three days, well." The family didn't believe it: They had heard things like that before.

This man went to the hospital—as it turned out, it was five hundred miles out of his way—and he found Jeannie. She said to Louise:

This kind-looking man came in and said, "I've come to pray for you." I was drugged and doing the only job I could do, which was to fill envelopes and lick them. He looked at me and I said, "I don't think there's any hope for me."

"Ah," he said. "The Lord just says to you, Isaiah 41:10: "Fear not, I am with you; be not dismayed."

My ears pricked up and I said, "That's the one verse I've leaned on for four years." I began to listen to him. He said, "I don't understand this, but the Lord wants me to tell you that he has never forgotten the eight-year-old girl who threw the pine cone into the fire and said she wanted to know Him personally."

I looked at him and said, "I've never told anybody that." He prayed for me.

The psychiatrist came to me the next day, and said, "Jeannie, what has happened to you?"

I said, "I'm healed, I want to go home."

He said, "You're not going home."

They put me through a battery of tests and they let me go home three days later just for the weekend. I never returned.

That was twenty years ago.

It began with a prophetic word, which at first would have been easy to dismiss. The man who prayed for Jeannie and gave her the prophetic word was Paul Cain. He happened to be at Westminster Chapel that Friday night while Jeannie Raborg was telling my wife her story. At the end of the evening, Paul got into the car with me, and before we had gone more than a few yards, he said, "Do you mind if I tell you something?"

I thought, *Uh-oh, here it comes*, but I said, "All right, yes."

He then shared something with me that was sobering. It was so right, so exact. Was I ready for that prophetic word? Maybe, maybe not. Are you ready for a prophetic word? There are four ways in which such a word might come.

1. Through an Unlikely Person

In January 1985, I had just finished preaching in Central Hall, Westminster, when a woman who was in the choir came down to the platform and said, "Could I just have a minute with you?"

I said, "Sure."

She said, "This week, as I was ironing, it hit me that I might see you this Saturday. And the Lord gave me a word for you."

And she gave it to me. It was so sweet, so wonderful; not quite like the word from Paul Cain that I described earlier. I thought, *Wow. I only hope it's true.* But she was just someone who had been ironing clothes. I thought, *Can I be sure that her word is right?* But I'll tell you this, I didn't treat it with contempt, and I keep hoping.

2. Through Preaching

Sometimes God will use me prophetically as I preach, and I don't have a clue that I'm saying something significant. I remember one day I began the service with 1 Corinthians 10:13, which says, "No temptation has seized you except what is common to man. And God is faithful; he will not let you be tempted beyond what you can bear. But when you are tempted, he will also provide a way out so that you can stand up under it."

A young lady in the service later said that the verse had hit her like a laser beam—she was convinced that I knew everything about her. I didn't; I didn't even know she was there. So God may use preaching. It may come at a lunchtime service; it may come at church on Sunday; it may come through a hymn.

"God was pleased through the foolishness of what was preached to save those who believe" (1 Corinthians 1:21). What if you were listening to the preaching of someone you didn't particularly like, when suddenly God got through to you? Would you think, *Wow! I didn't like him, but I like what he said?* After all, what matters is whether it's from God.

3. Through Reading the Bible

We all ought to be reading the Bible every day. And if we have a regular plan, God may use this to speak to us on a day when we're having a crisis. We may think, *He knew this was my reading. This is exactly what I needed.*

4. Through an Immediate and Direct Witness of the Spirit

I could count on one hand, I think, the times this has happened to me. The first instance was in April 1956, when I was in that severe crisis I described in chapter 7, and God put Philippians 1:12 into my mind out of the blue. I had no idea what that verse was until I pulled over the car, got out my Bible and read it. I can tell you now, that word held me for years and years. When you read it, you won't know why, but it was what I needed then.

So what is the purpose of the prophetic word?

To unveil God's secret will. The prophetic word unveils

God's secret will. It cuts across and yet is consistent with His revealed will—the Bible. It takes some time, but you do get to know God over the years through the Bible. It is an immature Christian who lives only for the prophetic word, who follows

THE BETTER YOU KNOW GOD'S WORD, THE MORE LIKELY IT IS YOU WILL BE GIVEN A PROPHETIC WORD.

around those who have the gift of prophecy. The chances are that a prophetic word will come only when you put the revealed will of God first.

Real devotion to Him is having a consistent Bible reading plan and getting regular teaching. When you know God well, you will discover that you almost instinctively know what is right and wrong and what to do. I believe, too, that the better you know God's Word, the more likely it is that you will get a prophetic word.

To encourage you. God's prophetic word will come in a time of crisis and will be exactly what you need. Such a word came to Paul: "Last night an angel of the God whose I am and whom I serve stood beside me and said, 'Do not be afraid, Paul. You must stand trial before Caesar; and God has graciously given you the lives of all who sail with you'" (Acts 27:23,24). In turn, Paul could say to the men on the ship, "So keep up your courage, men, for I have faith in God that it will happen just as he told me" (v. 25). Paul received God's word; he passed it on, and it was an encouragement.

God may give you a prophetic word to cheer you up. First Samuel 9:19,20—when Samuel finds the young Saul looking for his father's donkeys—is of interest here:

"I am the seer," Samuel replied. "Go up ahead of me to the high place, for today you are to eat with me, and in the morning I will let you go and will tell you all that is in your heart. As for the donkeys you lost three days ago, do not worry about them; they have been found. And to whom is all the desire of Israel turned, if not to you and all your father's family?"

That is the kind of word God can give—you are worried to death about something and He will send a prophet along to say, "It's okay."

To warn you. Sometimes this warning comes through the preached word, sometimes it comes from another person.

After we had been there a number of days, a prophet named Agabus came down from Judea. Coming over to us, he took Paul's belt, tied his own hands and feet with it and said, "The Holy Spirit says, 'In this way the Jews of Jerusalem will bind the owner of this belt and will hand him over to the Gentiles'" (Acts 21:10,11).

This was a warning to Paul to let him know what was going to happen in Rome.

A number of years ago, not long after I became minister at Westminster Chapel, our twelve deacons decided to do something that we all agreed was right. At the end of the meeting, after all the others had left, the senior deacon at the time stayed behind and said, "Dr. Kendall, about..."

I said, "Yes."

He said, "I believe you've been praying for unction."

That's all he said. I knew in that moment what he meant, and what I needed to do. It was a warning to stop the action decided on by the deacons, because it would probably have quenched the Spirit. I'm sure he was right to say what he did to me.

To give specific instructions. The Bible provides many examples of God giving a person or people specific instructions. Here is one:

When they [the Magi] had gone, an angel of the Lord appeared to Joseph in a dream. "Get up," he said, "take the child and his mother and escape to Egypt."

After Herod died, an angel of the Lord appeared in a dream to Joseph in Egypt and said, "Get up, take the child and his mother and go to the land of Israel, for those who were trying to take the child's life are dead" (Matthew 2:13,19).

What Kind of People Does God Use?

The answer is, anybody. Always be open.

However, what if God wants to raise you up to be someone who prophesies? Be prepared to be God's instrument to someone else. God may give *you* such a prophetic gift that people in the highest places will seek you out. God may tap you on the shoulder, giving you the word *from* someone *for* someone. If so, be prepared to be rejected, for the common experience of the prophet is that he or she is seldom received at first.

"Eagerly desire the greater gifts"; but then Paul says, "I will show you the most excellent way"—the way of love (1 Corinthians 12:31). "Follow the way of love and eagerly desire spiritual gifts, especially the gift of prophecy" (14:1).

Are you ready for that?

A
NEW PERSON IN
YOUR LIFE?

I asked the angel who talked with me, "What are these, my lord?"

He answered, "Do you not know what these are?"

"No, my lord," I replied.

So he said to me, "This is the word of the Lord to Zerubbabel: 'Not by *might nor by power, but by my Spirit,' says the Lord Almighty."

"What are you, O mighty mountain? Before Zerubbabel you will become level ground. Then he will bring out the capstone to shouts of 'God bless it! God bless it!'"

Then the word of the Lord came to me: "The hands of Zerubbabel have laid the foundation of this temple; his hands will also complete it. Then you will know that the Lord Almighty has sent me to you.

"Who despises the day of small things? Men will rejoice when they see the plumb line in the hand of Zerubbabel" (Zechariah 4:4-10).

Someone once said to me, "I don't have time for more friends. I know so many people that I literally don't have time for any new friends." I know what he meant. Perhaps you do, too. However, what if God planned to send someone into your life, someone who would change everything? Would you be ready?

It's extraordinary how God does this. A few years ago, we started doing something in Westminster Chapel that many other churches had been doing for years. We took a couple of minutes during the morning service to greet two or three people. Some members of the congregation were very hostile to the idea. I even had people coming to church late to make sure they got there after the greetings! Perhaps it was God's sense of humor, but relationships were made as a result. People discovered others they had never taken notice of before.

Shortly after Louise and I moved to Fort Lauderdale in 1958, I was invited to the house of the minister whose church we were attending. A man was there whom I had never met, and my friend the Reverend Jesse Oakley said, "R. T., I want you to meet Fred." When I looked at Fred, I immediately thought of a certain person I had known when I was a little boy. I'd never liked him. Poor Fred didn't have a chance! I decided he was just like that other person and I simply didn't want to meet him.

A few weeks later, I began to realize that God had sent this man, Fred Gowder, into our lives. It was he who introduced me to selling vacuum cleaners door-to-door, and our relationship turned out to be a pivotal, important one, though at first I had no idea of its value.

Selling vacuum cleaners for a living wasn't a very sophisticated job, and it didn't do a lot for my ego. However, during the time we lived in Fort Lauderdale, I had the opportunity to start a magazine—a spiritual, theological kind of journal called Redeemer's Witness. It had a mailing list of about a thousand people. Even working on this, I still felt unfulfilled and had no awareness of God's using me. However, six years later, when we had to move to Louisville, Kentucky, I got a phone call out of the blue from a man I had never met.

He said, "I hear you're coming to Louisville."

I said, "Yes, to go to seminary."

"I know," he said. "I'm pastor of a church across the river in Indiana. I'm giving it up—I'm leaving. Would you like me to recommend you to be the new pastor?"

Well, we hadn't known how we were going to make it financially at that time, and I certainly hadn't thought about God letting me be pastor of a church while I was in seminary. But it all worked out.

I asked the man, "By the way, how did you know me?"

He said, "I used to get Redeemer's Witness. That's how I knew you."

"Who despises the day of small things?"

When we came to England and were struggling financially again, out of the blue came a check, a substantial amount, from a lady I hardly knew. She had bought a vacuum cleaner from me ten years before. She had learned that I was at Oxford and had felt led to send the money.

After we had settled into Westminster Chapel, I was asked one day to go and see someone who lived around the corner. I couldn't see any importance in meeting this man, but I went, and at the very end of the conversation, he said, "Oh, by the way, Arthur Blessitt is here with me."

At that moment, Arthur came down the stairs! If I hadn't made the visit, I would have missed him. A couple of years later, we invited Arthur to Westminster Chapel, and I don't know where we would be today if it weren't for that man. As I've said already, he turned us upside down. So many good things have happened since, all because of that "chance" meeting.

God may bring someone into your life who gives you a shrewd word of wisdom. Years ago, when we were in Fort Lauderdale, I was explaining to a friend of mine in a restaurant that I was developing arthritis. I said, "You know, it even hurts to shake people's hands, and I don't know what I'm going to do."

SO MANY GOOD THINGS HAVE HAPPENED SINCE, ALL BECAUSE OF THAT "CHANCE" MEETING.

A lady came up to our table (as only Americans do) and said, "Excuse me, sir, I couldn't help overhearing your conversation. Take one teaspoonful of cod liver oil after your last meal every night for a year. Twenty-five years ago I couldn't tie my shoes. Now look at my hands." And she walked away. When I get to heaven I'll look her up. Or maybe she was an angel!

Why do you think God would send someone into your life? It may be for a special relationship. It may even be romantic. We read in Genesis 24:66:

> Then the servant told Isaac all he had done. Isaac brought her [Rebekah] into the tent of his mother Sarah, and he married Rebekah. So she became his wife, and he loved her; and Isaac was comforted after his mother's death.

God loves to bring men and women together. I have never been a good matchmaker—it makes my wife angry when I try. I

have only succeeded once, and I wish sometimes that I hadn't
then, so I stay out of it. But God is the matchmaker. God in His
sovereignty had Jacob be in a certain spot at a certain time:

> While he was still talking with them, Rachel came with her
> father's sheep, for she was a shepherdess. When Jacob saw
> Rachel...he went over and rolled the stone away from the
> mouth of the well and watered his uncle's sheep. Then Jacob
> kissed Rachel and began to weep aloud (Genesis 29:9-11).

I don't recommend you do that when you see someone you
think you're going to like! I don't know what Louise would have
done if I had walked into Olivet Nazarene College, where she had
a job while a student, and started to cry when I saw her. I don't
think it would have impressed her greatly. (Actually, nothing
impressed her at the time!) I pursued her—I mean, God sent me
into her life—and she didn't want me! Can you believe it? That
she should be so lucky! It seemed to take forever to win her, but
my dad used to pray for me, "Lord, don't let R. T. fall in love with
the wrong girl." That was a shrewd prayer because once you fall
in love, it's pretty hard to get out of it. God's hand was on me;
God's hand is on all of us, and He has a plan for you. That plan
may be marriage.

Or God may call you to a different kind of relationship.
Consider the story of Peter and Cornelius. When God brought
them together, it signaled the beginning of an era of which most
of us are a part today. Just as God had been gracious to the Jews,
so he was now gracious to Gentiles. Interestingly, Peter and
Cornelius were two people unlikely to meet, because it says in
Acts 10:28, "[Peter] said to them: 'You are well aware that it is
against our law for a Jew to associate with a Gentile or visit him.
But God has shown me that I should not call any man impure or
unclean.'" Be prepared for the person God sends not to be your
kind of person.

It may be a spiritual relationship.

Andrew, Simon Peter's brother, was one of the two who heard what John had said and who had followed Jesus. The first thing Andrew did was to find his brother Simon and tell him, "We have found the Messiah" (that is, the Christ). And he brought him to Jesus (John 1:40,41).

In Acts 18:24-26, we have the account of Apollos, the silver-tongued orator, knowledgeable in the Scriptures, who, nonetheless, needed some help from the Lord. Aquila and Priscilla heard him and they "invited him to their home and explained to him the way of God more adequately."

It may be a short relationship. When Philip entered into the life of the Ethiopian eunuch, it was only to lead him to Christ; then "the Spirit of the Lord suddenly took Philip away" (Acts 8:39). Be prepared for the one-off relationship that is life changing.

In 1963 we were living in Ohio. I was pastor of a church and I felt an utter failure. Then someone sent me Dr. Lloyd-Jones's book Sermon on the Mount. (I met him during the same year.) I read it at that low point in my life. Fourteen years later I showed Dr. Lloyd-Jones that book, which he had autographed for me, and I said, "Who would have thought in 1963 that I would be your pastor?" He then wrote in my Bible, quoting Romans 11:33 (from the King James Version): "How unsearchable are his judgments, and his ways past finding out!"

READY
FOR SUCCESS?

I will give you thanks, for you answered me; you have become my salvation.

The stone the builders rejected has become the capstone; the Lord has done this, and it is marvelous in our eyes.

This is the day the Lord has made; let us rejoice and be glad in it.

O Lord, save us; O Lord, grant us success.

Blessed is he who comes in the name of the Lord. From the house of the Lord we bless you.

The Lord is God, and he has made his light shine upon us. With boughs in hand, join in the festal procession up to the horns of the altar.

You are my God, and I will give you thanks; you are my God, and I will exalt you (Psalm 118:21-28).

One of the ways God appears—and it may seem a surprising one—is by giving us success. The psalmist prays, "O Lord, grant us success" (v. 25), but have you ever explicitly prayed for this? Do you think you are ready for it? If your answer is a quick yes, then I would caution you to be careful.

I used to sit at the feet of Dr. Lloyd-Jones—as I said before, I had the privilege of being his pastor for four years—and every Thursday I spent two hours with him discussing the sermon for the following Sunday. He once made this throwaway comment, and I immediately got my pen and wrote it down. It was the most powerful word I ever heard him say, yet it's in none of his books. I quote: "The worst thing that can happen to a man is to succeed before he is ready." It was a word of wisdom to me at the time.

If you do want success, do you think you are really ready for it?

In his book *The Price of Success*, J. B. Phillips tells how, in his own life, success was frequently followed by severe depression. There are those who have tasted success, yet have experienced such fallout from it that they wish they had never known it at all. It is easy to admire people who are jet-setters, who seem to have no financial problems, and to imagine what it must be like to be them. In fact, it has been my privilege to know some famous and wealthy people, and I have to say that I have yet to meet a person with whom I would trade places.

When I first came to Britain in 1973, the so-called "health and wealth" gospel was virtually unknown over here. Most people are probably familiar with it now—the idea that, if you are serving God as you should and you are pleasing Him in every way, you will be healthy and wealthy because God's will for you is health and wealth. But is that what the Bible teaches? Is there any truth in this "health and wealth" gospel?

The word "gospel" means "good news," and the thought that, if you come to Jesus Christ and please Him, He's going to heal you and make you rich is certainly good news! If that were the gospel of Jesus Christ, the apostle Paul would have been welcomed everywhere with open arms! But, when Paul went to Corinth, he said, "I resolved to know nothing while I was with you except Jesus Christ and him crucified" (1 Corinthians 2:2). He painted the worst possible picture. Why? Simply because the only way a person is going to be converted is through this gospel—that Jesus died on the cross for our sins; that He shed His blood, satisfying the justice of God so that we might be saved from His wrath. This is the gospel of the New Testament.

So is there anything at all to the health and wealth gospel? What about the Scripture verses its followers quote?

I must admit, I am attracted to Psalm 106:4,5, which reads: "Remember me, O Lord, when you show favor to your people,...that I may enjoy the prosperity of your chosen ones." This does indeed seem to be saying that, if you're one of God's elect, you're going to be prosperous. It almost seems to be saying that, if you are a Christian, part of the package is prosperity. Or take a verse like Deuteronomy 8:18: "Remember the Lord your God, for it is he who gives you the ability to produce wealth." Or Joshua 1:8: "Do not let this Book of the Law depart from your mouth; meditate on it day and night, so that you may be careful to do everything written in it. Then you will be prosperous and successful." That's encouraging, isn't it? I can understand why someone would take a verse like that, preach on it, and say, "If you do this, then God will do that."

Adherents of the prosperity gospel also point out that the gospel was first given to Abraham and that he was a "type" of the believer. What are we told about Abraham? In Genesis 24:35 his servant says, "The Lord has blessed my master abundantly, and he has become wealthy." Abraham was rich in possessions. So, too, was Isaac: "Isaac planted crops in that land and the same year reaped a hundredfold, because the Lord blessed him. The man became rich, and his wealth continued to grow until he became very wealthy" (Genesis 26:12,13). The same could be said of Jacob.

But these verses paint only a part of the picture. The truth is, God can make anybody wealthy. God could make any one of us a millionaire overnight, just by raising His little finger. But He can also withhold blessing. The apostle Paul says, "I know what it is to be in need, and I know what it is to have plenty. I have learned the secret of being content in any and every situation, whether well fed or hungry, whether living in plenty or in want" (Philippians 4:12).

Real Success

What is a balanced view of prosperity teaching? How about Psalm 75:2, where God says, "'I choose the appointed time; it is I who judge uprightly'"? Or, "No one from the east or the west or from the desert can exalt a man. But it is God who judges: he brings one down, he exalts another" (v. 6,7)? We need to know, at the end of the day, that we are in the hands of a sovereign God who could, if He wished, grant us all success.

GOD HAS A PLAN FOR EACH OF US.

As a minister, I watch other ministers succeed while I seem to stay at the same mediocre level. Yet some years ago, God made it clear that it was not His will for me to have any kind of lucrative sideline. I have friends in the ministry who have little things going on the side: I know one man who sometimes makes a lot more money from his sideline than he earns as a minister—and he has a greater anointing than I do! I think, *Lord, how could you do that? How could you give him that kind of power? You won't let me have it.*

And God says, "Be quiet. If I wanted to bless you, I could."

We have to come to terms with the fact that God has a plan for each of us, individually. God may grant us success: "The Lord will indeed give what is good" (Psalm 85:12); "no good thing does he withhold from those whose walk is blameless" (Psalm 84:11).

What kind of success are we talking about? It may well be prosperity. God does indeed give financial prosperity to some, though Christians who have wealth tend to come in for a certain amount of criticism that may spoil their enjoyment of it. However, once in a while, God will raise up a Joseph of Arimathea or a Lydia (see Matthew 27:57-60; Acts 16:14,15).

As I mentioned earlier, Louise and I came to England in 1973 without much idea of how we were going to manage financially. An old friend, Harlan Milby, promised to pay our way through Oxford—every penny of the tuition, all our costs. I took him fishing one day. When we were through, I said, "Tell me, how are you able to help people like this?" And he told me his story.

Many years ago he came across the Scripture verse, "'Those who honor me I will honor'" (1 Samuel 2:30). He made a covenant with God to give Him everything that was His and, he said, "I just kept the covenant." He was blessed. God knew that he could be trusted.

Then he told me about Bill, a man he got started in business. I had met Bill at university.

Harlan said, "We got him started in this business and he's been blessed; he's probably worth fifty million dollars today. If he wants a new suit, he doesn't buy it where he lives, he flies to London. And if he wants a nice weekend, he goes to New York."

I said, "How come you never set *me* up in business like that?"

He said, "Well, I've just never felt that's what you should do."

And I thought, *Well, if you really liked me, you could give me a break like that!*

Eighteen months later we were out fishing again, and I said, "Oh, by the way..." (I didn't really want to know the answer—I was just being courteous!) "...any news about Bill?"

"Oh," he said, "you haven't heard?"

I said, "No."

"Well, he's divorced, the Mafia are looking for him—I expect to hear that his body will be found buried in cement in the Atlantic Ocean somewhere. He's lost it all. He left God out of his life."

Later, Harlan wrote me a letter: "R. T., Bill chose the sand; you chose the rock."

I suppose Louise and I will never have a lot financially. But I reckon God has done me a great favor, because it's not something I've ever been ready for.

There are other kinds of success that God may give us. Have you longed to be promoted? Better job, better pay, better conditions? I watched my dad work for years as a rate clerk with the Chesapeake and Ohio Railway. We never had much. Different people would come up in the office and, even though Dad had worked there longer, they would be promoted and he wouldn't. It hurt. When Dad was finally promoted, it was wonderful and we rejoiced with him. I believe with all my heart that, when we are walking in the light, what is withheld from us is really a blessing that one day we'll appreciate more fully.

The Peter Principle

I often talk at Westminster Chapel about The Peter Principle, which is that everyone is promoted to the level of his or her incompetence. It happens again and again. The reason machines break down, the reason cars may not work, is that the person on the assembly line had a job that he wasn't able to do; he should have been sweeping floors. Or the person in management should have stayed on the assembly line instead of going into management, but she got moved up because a vacancy arose. Or perhaps someone was ambitious—he simply had to have that job—and now he can't think clearly, he has high blood pressure, his marriage is on the rocks—all because he got the job he wanted so much.

It may well be that you don't appreciate what you have now, and you may be envious of people who seem to have moved on. Some day you will find how good God has been to you. "'For I know the plans I have for you,'" declares the Lord, "'plans to prosper you and not to harm you, plans to give you hope and a future'" (Jeremiah 29:11). It could be that the kind of prosperity God has in mind is a little different from what you expected. "May he give you the desire of your heart and make all your plans succeed" (Psalm 20:4). But perhaps not quite in the way you had hoped.

The Best Success

Finally, I would like to stress that the greatest success of all you can ever have is not success in terms of prosperity or promotion, but success in prayer. One of the most moving verses in the Bible is Genesis 32:28, where Jacob wrestles with God:

> Then the man said, "Your name will no longer be Jacob, but Israel, because you have struggled with God and with men and have overcome."

God may want you to have influence with people, but how marvelous it would be if you could be trusted with a ministry of prayer. Some are more successful in prayer than others. Why? Because they want to be successful in prayer. I challenge you to make that your goal.

The worst thing that can happen to a person is to succeed before he's ready. But if you succeed because God says you're ready, there won't be that "after" of regret. You won't have been promoted to the level of your incompetence. If you succeed in prayer, you will have known a success greater than any other. Maybe books won't be written about you and you won't be buried at Westminster Abbey or have an obituary in *The Times*. But when you come to stand before God and Jesus Himself looks at you and says, "Well done!" it will be the greatest feeling and it will last forever.

READY
TO WITNESS?

While Paul was waiting for them in Athens, he was greatly distressed to see that the city was full of idols. So he
reasoned in the synagogue with the Jews and the God-
fearing Greeks, as well as in the marketplace day by day
with those who happened to be there. A group of
Epicurean and Stoic philosophers began to dispute with
him. Some of them asked, "What is this babbler trying to
say?" Others remarked, "He seems to be advocating for-
eign gods." They said this because Paul was preaching the
good news about Jesus and the resurrection. Then they
took him and brought him to a meeting of the Areopagus,
where they said to him, "May we know what this new
teaching is that you are presenting? You are bringing some
strange ideas to our ears, and we want to know what they
mean" (Acts 17:16-20).

What if the way God chose to appear in your life was to say, "From now on, I want you to stop being ashamed of me, and to tell people that you're saved, and warn people that *they* need to be saved. You must be a witness"?

One difference between the apostle Paul and me (!) is that Paul was ready for God to talk to him like that, and I wasn't. In fact, I think I have uncovered the secret of Paul being a great theologian: he loved to preach to the lost, not just from a pulpit or in a synagogue, but wherever he happened to be. In Acts 17:17 we read, "So he reasoned in the synagogue with the Jews and the God-fearing Greeks, as well as in the marketplace day by day with those who happened to be there."

Paul is waiting for Silas and Timothy in Athens. Athens would be a great place to visit. I can think of no greater place to be if you don't know what to do. I would want to go to the Parthenon; I would want to see the sights. Paul is "waiting for them," but his heart is stirred by the idolatry he sees and he decides to make use of the time. He "reasoned in the synagogue." You might think, *Well, that's fine because that's his calling. It's easy to understand him going to the synagogue.* But that wasn't all. He "reasoned in the synagogue...as well as in the marketplace day by day with those who happened to be there." The people in the marketplace weren't expecting somebody to come up to them and start talking about Jesus Christ.

Pilot Lights

When I finished my studies at Oxford, I didn't expect to be called to a church in England. We were planning to go straight back to the United States. However, I was asked to preach at Westminster Chapel, and I have been there ever since. As I said earlier, I was sure I was prepared at that stage to do what God had called me to do. I had just had my thesis published and hoped that I was going to be a theologian of world class.

I was having a good ministry at Westminster Chapel. It ticked along nicely for about five years. There were no real problems, and I had invitations to preach all over Britain. Then I invited Arthur Blessitt to the Chapel. I know that I have mentioned Arthur before, but let me tell you the story of what happened more fully. Arthur was what some would call the "father of the Jesus Movement" and people were offended at the thought of him coming. I knew it was right to have him, and not only did I invite him to preach, but, after hearing him once or twice, I also pleaded with him on bended knee to stay with us for a whole month in 1982. All I wanted was to have him preach. But then he said, "Well, we've got to be out on the streets witnessing."

I said, "Fine. I'll tell you what we'll do, Arthur. Friday night I'll have you address our young people, and then we'll all go to Page Street—a fifteen minute walk from here—and we'll witness."

"Fine," he said.

Thirty or forty of our young people came into what we used to call the Church Parlor, and Arthur fired them up. We were ready to go and evangelize. As was our habit, we started off for Page Street, because that's the only place in Westminster where you can knock on people's doors. All the other places have entry phones and you can't get in. On Page Street, people come right to the door. We usually took a little survey sheet with us, asked the people a few questions and then maybe invited them to church. That was our way of doing door-to-door evangelism. We knew of no other.

We started out, everybody heading for Page Street. We were all excited. But as soon as Arthur got to the end of the yard, he saw three young people at the zebra crossing. He went right up to them. I said, "Arthur, look, we've got to get to Page Street."

He said, "Just a minute, Dr. Kendall."

He started talking to these three young people and, do you know, two of them were interested. About twenty minutes later they prayed to receive the Lord! There I was, just watching and saying, "Arthur we've got to get to Page Street."

Then Arthur took several more minutes with the follow-up. He got out another pamphlet explaining what had just happened to them and what to do now: read the Bible and witness, pray every day, things like that. Then finally he finished. I said, "Arthur, we need to go."

UNTIL YOU'RE READY TO TALK TO ONE PERSON, YOU'RE NOT READY TO TALK TO HUNDREDS.

Arthur said, "Just a minute." A young man was coming from the other direction and he went right to him. I happened to know who that man was, and I thought, *Well, this is interesting. He stopped coming to the Chapel two years ago.*

Soon Arthur had him on his knees! The man surrendered to the Lord. Then Arthur turned to me and said, "Dr. Kendall, I don't know where this Page Street is, but you don't need to leave the steps of your church!"

In that moment, I had what I think might have been a vision. I could see a pilot light—like the light in a stove that stays lit twenty-four hours a day. I knew right then that I would have to start witnessing on the streets. I envisaged some of us going out every Saturday to talk to people, whoever they were, and I thought of the old hymn we used to sing back in the hills of Kentucky, which had a phrase, "My ambitions, plans and wishes"—theologian, world-class—"my ambitions, plans and wishes at His feet in ashes lay." I knew I had to become a fool for Christ.

We started the next Saturday after Arthur had left us. I was so fired up to talk to people about the Lord that, if no one else had shown up—six people did—I would have gone by myself. For thirteen years now, I've not missed a Saturday if I'm in London. We have seen things happen that you wouldn't believe. But then, I know we have been doing what the apostle Paul would have done. He was the greatest theologian in the history of the world, yet he was willing to witness in the marketplace, not just in the synagogue. He didn't know who he would be talking to, there was no prior arrangement. It was spontaneous.

I knew a man who felt called into the ministry. I said to him, "Well, why don't you test that by joining us on the streets and talking to the lost?"

He said, "I could preach to hundreds, but I couldn't talk to one person."

I said, "Until you're ready to talk to one person, you're not ready to talk to hundreds."

Before this, I had never done street witnessing in my life! I always felt that I was doing my bit by preaching evangelistic sermons on Sunday nights and, if I preached the gospel, that was my "being an evangelist." But God showed up in my life that Friday night when we were all going to Page Street. I wasn't ready for it. I had wanted to see something happen, but not like that. What about you?

Making the Opportunity

I learned something else from this story of Paul. Five years ago, when we were on a Mediterranean cruise, one of our stops was Athens. We all went to Mars Hill and, while we were there, I read the verses at the beginning of this chapter. I realized something I had never thought of before. Paul had an opportunity to speak at the Areopagus (the hill to the northwest of the Acropolis where the Athenian judicial council met) to the philosophers of the day. He would never have had this opportunity if he had first gone to the Areopagus and said, "I'm Saul of Tarsus. I would like to address you."

The fact is, Paul wasn't trying to get to the Areopagus. He was witnessing in the marketplace to anyone who happened to be there, and it turned out that some people from the Areopagus were doing their shopping just then. Paul didn't know who they were, but he started talking to them and, as a result, they brought him to the Areopagus and said, "Speak to us."

Sometimes when a person tries too hard to get onto a particular platform, he won't make it. "'Whoever tries to keep his life will lose it, and whoever loses his life will preserve it'" (Luke 17:33). But when he *doesn't* try, God may put him there. By being nothing, Paul had a door opened to one of the highest places of all.

Visitors to Athens today will find a bronze plaque at the foot of Mars Hill. Inscribed on it is none other than the sermon Paul preached. The "big names" of those who frequented the Areopagus have vanished into history. There is nothing to commemorate them—only Paul and what he said. All because he was willing to witness "in the marketplace."

Wherever You Happen to Be

You may wonder what's happened to me since those days with Arthur Blessitt. I have gained much greater insight into Scripture than I ever had before. I have learned things that they can't teach you at Oxford, things that you don't learn from a book about theology. Do you know why? Paul said to Philemon, "I pray that you may be active in sharing your faith, so that you will have a full understanding of every good thing we have in Christ" (Philemon 6).

Do *you* want to know how to have a deeper knowledge of the Bible? "Be active in sharing your faith." God may appear today and say, "This is the way I want to use you."

As a result of what we did thirteen years ago, all the invitations to preach I had been getting came to an abrupt end. The constituency we had previously known wanted to have nothing to do with me. For a year or two we were in no-man's-land. However, some time after we started going out and witnessing on the streets, people began to realize that we were sincere. I began to get an invitation here or there. That vision of the pilot light eventually led me to places I could never have gone before. And, of course, it has led us to people we would probably never have met.

In 1994, I received a letter from Moscow from a lady by the name of Luba. She was walking down Buckingham Gate. I didn't know who she was or that she was Russian—she spoke fairly good English. She stopped and talked, and forty-five minutes later I led her to Christ. In her letter, she said, "That was the happiest day of my life." Now she's witnessing to people in her office and she wants more literature.

Before I end this chapter, I should tell you about a little problem we had at home. Louise wasn't sure that I ought to be out on the streets witnessing, and she wasn't sure that we ought to be training people in Evangelism Explosion—at least, she didn't feel *she* needed it because, as she said, "I've sat under your ministry for twenty-five years; surely that's taught me something!"

However, one Saturday morning, Louise said, "I'm going out today as a Pilot Light."

I said, "Great!"

What I didn't know was that she had asked God for a sign that this was what she was supposed to be doing. She found herself at St. James's tube station. A young man wearing a Che Guevara T-shirt came up to her and said, "What are you selling?"

She said, "I...I don't suppose you want one of these pamphlets?"

He took one. It was called *What is Christianity?*

He looked at her, and tears filled his eyes. He said, "I'm a Marxist, an atheist. But five minutes ago, I was in a church, and I said, 'God, if you're really there, let me run into somebody who believes in you.'" Then he looked at her and said, "I've got to get a train. You've got five minutes to convert me." And she didn't know what to say! Sitting under my ministry for twenty-five years, and she didn't know what to say!

When I asked Arthur Blessitt to come and preach, I didn't like the way God showed up, but it changed my life and I became just a little more like the apostle Paul. Not just a theologian, but also an evangelist, and not just an evangelist in the pulpit, but wherever I happen to be.

THE
SECOND COMING

"No one knows about that day or hour, not even the angels in heaven, nor the Son, but only the Father. As it was in the days of Noah, so it will be at the coming of the Son of Man. For in the days before the flood, people were eating and drinking, marrying and giving in marriage, up to the day Noah entered the ark; and they knew nothing about what would happen until the flood came and took them all away. That is how it will be at the coming of the Son of Man. Two men will be in the field; one will be taken and the other left. Two women will be grinding with a hand mill; one will be taken and the other left.

"Therefore keep watch, because you do not know on what day your Lord will come. But understand this: If the owner of the house had known at what time of night the thief was coming, he would have kept watch and would not have let his house be broken into. So you also must be ready, because the Son of Man will come at an hour when you do not expect him" (Matthew 24:36-44).

The Second Coming has been very special to me for as long as I can remember, even when I was a little boy. One night, coming out of our church in Ashland, Kentucky, the moon was red. My father commented, "Look at the moon. Do you realize that the Bible says that when the moon is the color of oxblood, it's a sign of the second coming of Jesus?" I was terrified. When I got home that night, I lay in bed and confessed every sin I could think of before I let myself fall asleep. Later, as I grew up, I realized that the moon that night had been in the direction of the steel mill, and it was smoke that had caused it to look red!

I remember another occasion when I was up on the roof of a house that was being repaired, and there was the most beautiful white fluffy cloud in the sky. One of the men on the roof, a former pastor, said, "Look at that cloud. I reckon that's the kind of cloud Jesus will be on when He comes back again." I almost fell off the roof! I got myself down, found a secret place and confessed every sin I could think of—again!

As far back as I can remember, the Second Coming has gripped me.

We have been looking at the subject of being ready for God— being ready for Him to appear unexpectedly and in any number of ways—but the subject of this chapter is rather different. First, there is no way we will be able to miss the Second Coming, though it will come unexpectedly. Second, we do know a certain amount about how the Lord will appear, when He comes again, from what the Bible tells us.

Matthew 24:44 says, "'Be ready, because the Son of Man will come at an hour when you do not expect him.'" He may not come in my lifetime, although I will not be surprised if He does. I am convinced that we are very, very close to the second coming of

Jesus, and yet I don't want to make the mistake of some who have been so convinced that the Lord was coming in their day that they went so far as to say that God had told them when. I knew a sweet couple in Tennessee who said God witnessed to them that they would be alive at the time of the Second Coming. They died thirty years ago. But they sincerely thought they would see Jesus come again.

The truth is, we don't know if Jesus will come in our day, and yet we are told that He will come when we don't expect Him. So if we don't expect the second coming of Jesus today, today is a day He might well come. Peter put it like this in 2 Peter 3:3:

> In the last days scoffers will come, scoffing and following their own evil desires. They will say, "Where is this 'coming' he promised? Ever since our fathers died, everything goes on as it has since the beginning of creation."

Perhaps you have heard cynical people say, "Second Coming? Ha! I've heard it all before! He hasn't come yet." Just remember, their use of that very language is in itself a fulfillment of Peter's prophecy.

ARE WE READY FOR JESUS TO COME AGAIN TODAY?

I don't know why the Lord has delayed His coming, but I'm sure it's for a good reason. I can tell you honestly that I'm glad He didn't come a hundred years ago, because I wouldn't have been born. I'm glad He didn't come before April 5, 1942, because

I wouldn't have been saved. Some of you reading this wouldn't have been ready two years ago if He had come then. Some of us have loved ones who are not yet saved, so the very fact that He hasn't come yet should be cause for gladness. This apart, are we ready to echo John when, having been given a sneak preview of the whole event, he concluded the book of Revelation with these words, "Come, Lord Jesus"? Are we ready for Him to come again today?

In Matthew 24:45-51, Jesus says:

> "Who then is the faithful and wise servant, whom the master has put in charge of the servants in his household to give them their food at the proper time? It will be good for that servant whose master finds him doing so when he returns. I tell you the truth, he will put him in charge of all his possessions. But suppose that servant is wicked and says to himself, 'My master is staying away a long time,' and he then begins to beat his fellow servants and to eat and drink with drunkards. The master of that servant will come on a day when he does not expect him and at an hour he is not aware of. He will cut him to pieces and assign him a place with the hypocrites, where there will be weeping and gnashing of teeth."

The Fact of the Second Coming of Jesus

Now, I suppose the strongest language in the New Testament, which shows without any doubt what the Bible means by the second coming of Jesus, is recorded in Acts 1:10,11:

> They were looking intently up into the sky as he [Jesus] was going, when suddenly two men dressed in white stood beside them. "Men of Galilee," they said, "why do you stand here looking into the sky? This same Jesus, who has

been taken from you into heaven, will come back in the same way you have seen him go into heaven."

This is a literal event of Jesus personally, physically, bodily, coming back in the same way He personally, physically, bodily went into heaven. Yet a number of wrong interpretations of the Second Coming have emerged in the history of the Christian Church.

The Prophecy Was Fulfilled at Pentecost
Some have said that, because Jesus hasn't returned as soon as they expected, this prophecy has been misinterpreted, and the fulfillment of it actually came at Pentecost in the person of the Holy Spirit.

What might we say to that? First, Acts 1:11 says, "This same Jesus...will come back in the same way." And throughout the book of Acts, Jesus' followers are still looking for His return.

The Second Coming of Jesus Happens at Conversion
The first time Jesus came, He was born of a virgin. He lived for thirty-three years, died on a cross and rose from the dead. He comes a second time when we are saved and He enters into our hearts.

What might we say about this? Simply, that Acts 1:11 says, "This same Jesus...will come back in the same way you have seen him go into heaven." Jesus doesn't literally come into our hearts; it's the Holy Spirit, the Spirit of Christ, who comes into our hearts, who makes Jesus real.

The Second Coming of Jesus Is Death
This view says, "You do not know the day or the hour—you are to be ready. And when you die the Lord comes for you."

Again, the Scriptures make it clear that this is *not* the Second Coming. Everybody must die: "Man is destined to die once, and after that to face judgment" (Hebrews 9:27); then, says verse 9:28, Christ will come. So don't think for a moment that it's simply death. We're talking about a literal, historic event. It will be a place on the map—don't ask me where; it will be a date in history—don't ask me when! But He's coming.

The Second Coming Is the Growth of the Church

Some have taken the view that the second coming of Jesus was simply spreading Christianity, spreading His Word around the world. Why, then, does the book of Revelation, written perhaps in A.D. 90-100, still talk about the second coming of Jesus? Because it is to be a literal event.

The Manner of the Second Coming

What can we say about the way Jesus will come again? Two things:

1. When Jesus comes, He will come *suddenly*. "'I am coming soon'" (Revelation 22:7). First Corinthians 15:51,52 says, "I tell you a mystery: We will not all sleep, but we will all be changed—in a flash, in the twinkling of an eye, at the last trumpet. For the trumpet will sound, the dead will be raised imperishable, and we will be changed."

The words that say "in a flash, in the twinkling of an eye" come from a Greek word that shows Jesus' coming will happen more quickly than you can bat an eyelash. Suddenly, when it happens, He's here! No more opportunity to be converted. I'll tell you one thing, if you're not converted, you will pray *then* like you should pray *now*. It will be one awesome event, when people will lose their sense of pride, their sense of dignity—it won't matter who is around—they will look up and see He's there, because "every eye will see him" (Revelation 1:7). And they will pray, they will scream, they will wail, they will cry out, "Oh my God, save me! Save me! Mercy!"

You will pray like that then. I would urge you to pray like that now, while there is hope. For He will come, according to 2 Peter 3:10, "like a thief." It will be unexpected and sudden.

2. When Jesus comes, He will come "with the clouds." I mentioned earlier that when my old pastor saw big beautiful white cumulus clouds, they made him think of the kind of clouds Jesus would come on. It does say again and again that He comes with clouds. Now some have thought that this means clouds of angels, or a mist, perhaps the sun, I don't know.

As for the time of His coming, only the Father knows. Matthew 24:36: "'No one knows about that day or hour, not even the angels in heaven, nor the Son, but only the Father.'" One thing is for sure, it is fixed, and in the future. If you are not saved, thank God there is time. I don't know how much time, but if I didn't know for sure that I was ready to meet the Lord, I would not let the sun set this day.

"Even so, come, Lord Jesus" (Revelation 22:20, *KJV*).